The Song of
Girart of Vienne
by Bertrand de Bar-Sur-Aube

MEDIEVAL & RENAISSANCE

TEXTS & STUDIES

VOLUME 196

The Song of
Girart of Vienne
by Bertrand de Bar-Sur-Aube

A TWELFTH-CENTURY CHANSON DE GESTE

Translated by

Michael A. Newth

Arizona Center for Medieval and Renaissance Studies
Tempe, Arizona
1999

Library of Congress Cataloging-in-Publication Data

Girard de Viane (Chanson de geste). English
    The song of Girart of Vienne by Bertrand de Bar-sur-Aube : a twelfth-century chanson de geste / translated by Michael A. Newth.
        p. cm. — (Medieval & Renaissance Texts & Studies ; v. 196)
    Includes bibliographical references.
    ISBN 0-86698-238-8
    1. Chansons de geste—Translations into English. 2. Epic poetry, French—Translations into English.   I. Bertrand de Bar-sur-Aube, 12th cent.
II. Newth, Michael A. III. Title. IV. Series: Medieval & Renaissance Texs & Studies (Series) ; v. 196.
PQ1463.G78E5 1999
841'.1—dc21   99–17134
                                                                                              CIP

For Clifford Aspland

"Deus et seint Pere vos en sache bon gré
de cest avoir que nos avez presté;"

Girart de Vienne ll. 404–405

Contents

Introduction

Authorship

The *chanson de geste* known today as *Girart de Vienne* is preserved in five manuscript copies, four of them part of large cyclic compilations, which date from the middle of the thirteenth to the middle of the fourteenth centuries. The poem itself is considered by its most recent editor, Wolfgang Van Emden (1977), to have been composed around the year 1180, and it remains of first importance, both historically and artistically, to the study of baronial revolt as it appears in the Old French epics written during the reign of King Philippe-Auguste (1180–1222) of France. *Girart de Vienne* is also a poem of pivotal significance generically, as it establishes and itself forms a link among the three main cycles of contemporary and subsequent *chanson de geste* composition—a feat achieved through the author's highly original and influential recreation of the life, family relationships, and bellicose exploits of a leading Carolingian nobleman.

Gerardus (819–877), count of Vienne in the Dauphiné region of southeastern France, played an important role in the struggles of the regional barons against the Normans in Provence during the latter stages of the reign of Charlemagne's son, Louis the Pious, and that of his successor King Charles the Bald. In the year 870 Count Gerardus was beseiged by King Charles in Vienne and, although he was forced into an eventual retreat, his heroic stand before the king's forces soon made him a legendary symbol of local resistance to the arrogant but weakening Frankish monarchy. From the moment of his exile in Avignon to his death and interment at Pothières—where, as at Vézelay, he and his wife Bertha had founded a monastery—there is evidence to suggest that popular chants lamenting his misfortune and extolling his stubbornness had already sprung into existence. Scholars such as A. Longnon (1878) and R. Louis (1947) have traced the spread of these chants from the foothills of the Pyrenees along the length of the Rhône valley to the northernmost limits of Burgundy. An elaborate oral and written tradition surrounding the count was fostered and developed particularly in the antiroyalist enclaves of Burgundy, Dauphiné, and Provence. Gerardus became known variously as Girart of Roussillon, of Vienne, and of Fraite (or of Eufrate), as the first epics in his honor proceeded to confuse and then consciously fuse geographical and biographical fact and fiction in their regional exploitations of his name and his fame.

Only one other *chanson de geste* having Girart as its central character has come down to us today—*Girart de Roussillon*, thought to have been written around 1150. This poem and other surviving epics featuring Girart offer substantial internal evidence of narrative composition within a well-established framework of traditional "Girart material," inherited from earlier *chansons de geste*. These works, if ever they were written down, are lost to us now. There is, however, sufficient testimony from the considerable corpus of Old French epic writing which has survived, as well as from later collections in verse and prose of the epic materials of French and other European writers, to indicate that during the tenth and eleventh centuries a change in Count Girart's legendary status took place. It is clear from a perusal of the extant epics that even as his name crystallized in the national imagination to become that of a powerful peer of Charlemagne's, so his most famous exhibition of this power was pared down provincially to a popular representation of Girart as an arrogant baron, whose refusal to render vassalage to his liege-lord had led him into treason and even into apostasy. Both the *Chanson de Roland* and the *Chançun de Willame*, two of the oldest extant epics, make mention of Girart as of a figure well known to their audiences. In the *Roland*, as Gerard de Russilon, one of the Twelve Peers of Charlemagne, he is mentioned four times and three times referred to as "the old." In the *Willame* he is known as Girard de Viane and we are told that William's jongleur sings of him and of Oliver "who were his (i.e., William's) relations and ancestors." In *Girart de Vienne* the poet specifies Girart as the uncle of Aymeri (and hence as the great-uncle of William of Orange) and of Oliver and Aude (Roland's betrothed), but his general relationship to these, the most famous and beloved characters in the Old French epic tales, seems to have been well established in the popular mind by at least the beginning of the twelfth century. Radulfus Tortarius (d. 1114) for one, records his knowledge of it. Nevertheless it is a negative conception of Girart as an arrogant and disloyal baron which pervades the mid-twelfth century *Girart de Roussillon*, and the much earlier and now lost major source poem(s) for the present composition, referred to by scholars variously as the *Chanson de*

Vaubeton, *Girart de Fraite* or indeed *Girart de Vienne*, the contents of which are known to us through the records of the Scandinavian *Karlamagnus Saga* (1230–50) and the *Chronique Rimée* (c.1260) of Philippe Mousket. The *Chanson d'Aspremont*, probably written in the same decade as *Girart de Vienne* itself, presents the count also in this unfavorable light, as a rebellious baron without a real cause. It is against this background, therefore, that the intent and originality of the author of the present work, Bertrand de Bar-sur-Aube, should be appreciated and understood. He tells his audience (ll. 81–89) that although they have heard Girart's story often enough from other singers (meaning doubtless the story of his insubordination) only he, Bertrand, is aware of its origins *"la començaille dont la chançon oisi."* It is clear from what follows that his artistic purpose is to cast his rebellious hero in a much more favorable light. He achieves this by giving to his source poem(s) a moral bias which will typify the epics of baronial revolt.

Girart de Vienne is one of the very few *chansons de geste* in which the author identifies himself. In lines 91–101 he gives his name as *Bertrans*, describes himself as a *gentis clers* (noble clerk), and says that he wrote down this song while sitting in a budding grove of the noble town Bar-sur-Aube. The language and dialectical traits discernible in the versification of the poem we possess are indeed those of a cultured Champenois. At the end of his work he announces that his next song will recount the deeds of Aymeri of Narbonne:

> Et de son fiz ci après vos diron:
> C'est d'Aymeri qui tant par fu proudom,
> Le seignor de Nerbone.
>
> ll. 6927–29

Although such "linkage verses" are common in works of cyclic compilation—indeed, sometimes the initiative of the scribal hand—the actual poem of *Aymeri de Narbonne* succeeds *Girart de Vienne* in three of the four cyclic manuscripts extant, and most scholarly and literary research has concluded that Bertrand de Bar is the author of this second work also. It appears that Bertrand de Bar-sur-Aube, little known today, was a *trouvère* of some celebrity at the turn of the thirteenth century. The author of the *chanson de geste* called *Doon de Nanteuil*, for example, which dates from that period, can best praise another *jongleur* by stating that "he learnt more in a single year than Bertrand de Bar did in his whole life." Although all biographical details concerning Bertrand remain conjectural, two further epics which have come down to us, the

Département des Enfants d'Aymeri (which forms the first half of the *chanson de geste* known nowadays as *Les Narbonnais*) and one version of *Beuve de Hantone* have also been attributed to him by most scholars. That this noble clerk, whose skills in the composition of the more subtle and reflective narrative typical of the *roman courtois* are evidenced in all these poems, must have traveled widely in the south of France is indicated not only by his attested fame in Gascony and Provence particularly, but also by the frequency, variety, and accuracy of the topographical references to the Midi region which he makes in his works. That he may have also enjoyed the patronage of the court of Champagne under Henry the Liberal and the Countess Marie has also been considered (Benton, 1959). Van Emden has also suggested a connection between the composition of *Girart de Vienne* (a poem written by a Champagne poet in praise of a Burgundian duke) and the marriage of Henry and Marie's daughter Scholastique to William, the son of Girart I of Vienne and Mâcon. In the political atmosphere of the coalition against Philippe-Auguste, which began in the years 1181–83, it is known that the house of Champagne took several steps to align itself with this contemporary rebel Girart. It is certain that Bertrand's poem, where the responsibility for civil war is thrown back upon an indecisive, ungrateful, and vindictive monarch, would have prospered at such a moment.

Artistic Achievement

In *Girart de Vienne* Bertrand de Bar has created an interesting range of psychologically credible characters whose relations, both cordial and hostile, are depicted with considerable dramatic and comic skill. His narrative is well crafted, varied in style, and centered on a strong and fresh conception of the protagonist. The author has also created an influential work that consciously constructs a bridge between the William of Orange and Charlemagne cycles of epics by providing a prologue or *enfances* poem which interrelates for the first time the principal characters of each, e.g., Roland and Oliver, Roland and Aude, Charlemagne and Aymeri, and, of course, Girart and them all.

Bertrand's portrayal of Girart as the ideal liegeman and lord, "well-bred and brave," an epitome of the courtly and the chivalric ideal, is carefully and consistently maintained with deft allusion and open illustration throughout the entire poem. It serves both as the measure against which the qualities of all the other characters are to be judged and as the mainspring of the personality conflicts that advance the composition. Throughout the first and most original section of the poem Girart, although the youngest of Garin de Monglane's four sons, is clearly distinguished as the "first among equals." It is his plan to waylay a Saracen caravan which subsequently relieves his father's sufferings at the hands of Sinagon the Moor. It is Girart who in a famous speech deplores the use of the bow as being a cowardly weapon for knightly combat, and who, as the poet directly says, "boasts the least, but his deeds speak the most." When he and his brother Renier are received most condescendingly by the arrogant barons and toadying courtiers in Paris, and when their subsequent services go virtually unrewarded, it is Girart who continually strives to keep the peace between his increasingly insubordinate elder brother and an increasingly arrogant Charlemagne. Girart's steady loyalty to the church and the state is contrasted sharply with the emperor's selfish whim in marrying the widowed duchess, whose hand he had promised to Girart, and with the duchess' own opportunist acceptance of the emperor and the capricious and malicious revenge she exacts upon Girart's forthright probity. The new queen's insulting treachery, when she tricks Girart into setting the kiss of fealty upon her foot instead of on the king's, is the author's original narrative justification for the legendary hostility between Charlemagne and Girart. It is Charlemagne's unwillingness to punish the queen, which as Girart's liege-lord he is bound to do, which puts him fairly and squarely in the wrong.

During the long course of the siege of Vienne, and even more so in the scene which brings it to a conclusion, Bertrand adds subtly and ingeniously to the moral weight of Girart's cause. For example, whereas Charles is intransigent in his demand for Girart's submission and even death, Girart himself is devastated to discover that he has mistakenly struck his liege, the king, during one of the skirmishes outside Vienne. He even sends his beloved nephew Oliver to Charles's camp in the company of Lanbert of Berry (the emperor's captured but freely released godson) to justify his right to rule Vienne through hereditary claim—but their embassy is met with royal rebuke and violence. The long single combat which ensues between Oliver and Roland transposes the moral balance of the conflict exactly but not simply onto a physical plane—for the counts are both the human and idealised champions of their respective causes, whose opposition requires a metaphysical resolution, inspired by divine love, to be found. The introduction of young Aymeri as Girart's other nephew provides the narrative with a more down-to-earth avenue of human appeal and is, perhaps, the artistic master-stroke of the poem. First, enormous prestige and sympathy are added to Girart's character and cause among the audience through this alignment with the famous father of the even more famous William of Orange and all his much-loved *geste*. Second, the fiery Aymeri's character provides a credible catalyst to the final progressions of the plot. Third, his rash actions illustrate by contrast the virtues of the more temperate Girart. For example, the uncle first urges his ebullient nephew to serve in Charles's court, as he himself had done, affirming:

> You could not lodge in any finer place
> Than Charles's court, whose honor is so great,
> And who has raised us all through his own fame
> And through his gifts of lands and great estates.
>
> ll. 1690–93

Then it is Aymeri who, discovering the insult of the queen's deceit, and reacting most violently in its revenge, jeopardizes the reconciliation that Girart eventually seeks. He slays a royal office-bearer and urges the torture and slaughter of Charlemagne, when the emperor is caught at last in a clever ambush. When this, the real climax of the poem, is reached, it is Girart the "rebel" whose personal solution to the secular struggles between Paris and the provinces most closely resembles the divine resolution proffered earlier. By submitting the personal compromise of a vassal wronged as a challenge to the honor of a monarchy at fault he gains the ultimate moral victory over the king. To the hot-headed Aymeri's pleas for revenge, in the presence of all, he replies:

> May God forbid the deed!
> A King of France shall not be harmed by me!
> If he forgives me, I'll be his man of liege
> And hold from him all of my lands in fief;
> If he will not, by blessèd St. Maurice,
> I shall depart for Arab lands and leave;
> I shall be shamed and men shall lose esteem
> For our Emperor's honor.
>
> ll. 6416–23

Neither that of the idealized patriarch of the earliest epics nor that of the burlesque graybeard of some later poems, the character of Charlemagne in *Girart de Vienne* is carefully constructed to serve as both a functionary and foil to that of Duke Girart himself. As a result the portrait of the emperor which gradually emerges in the narrative is one of the best of him in Old French epic writing, presenting a much more credible mixture of human strengths and weaknesses against which those of Girart can be weighted and consequently weighed. He is shown to be both majestic and foolish, an unwavering ruler of many but an unstable wooer of one—generous, mean, conciliatory, antagonistic, humorous, and somber. He is openly brave and caring for his beloved queen and nephew Roland, while the former deceives and embarrasses him and the latter blames him for starting the war with Girart and for showing poor military tactics in its conduct. On the other hand Girart's wife, Guibourc (true, no doubt, to her prototype and namesake Orable/Guibourc, wife of William of Orange), is a reliable partner, religious, loyal, supportive, and enterprising, while his nephews Oliver and Aymeri are unwavering and uncritical in their uncle's support. Both Charlemagne and Girart are high-hearted and high-handed in their dealings with each other and with others in their courts, but it is Charles's breach of faith, his broken promise of the duchess's hand, and even more his failure to avenge his liegeman's humiliation at her hands, which prove and move the moral balance of the pair at war.

Some of the finest and funniest verses of Bertrand's poem are those in which he relates his version of the *enfances* or youthful exploits of several of the genre's most famous individuals or pairs. Part of his artistic purpose in doing this lies undoubtedly in his desire to produce a work which might stand at the narrative heart of the genre's cyclic productions by interrelating the principal characters of the *gestes* of the king, of Doon of Mayence (or rebel barons), and of Garin of Monglane (or William of Orange), as expressed in his famous prologue. These narrative excursions are equally a means of deepening and lightening the basically simple and somber texture of his work, to widen its appeal by introducing some traditional and original motifs and episodes of humor, romance, and social criticism. The ready fists and tongues of Garin's sons, for example, particularly those of Renier and Girart, shock both the refined sensibilities and physical senses of Charles's Parisian courtiers. Their regional pride and much of the spirited sarcasm with which they express it produce moments ranging from slapstick comedy to antiélitist diatribe, both extremes balanced by the egalitarian notion found time and again in *chansons de geste* of this era, that:

> The heart's not clad in gray or ermine clothes
> But in the breast where God grants that it grow.
>
> ll. 607–608

Considerable "generation-gap" humor is present in many of the dialogues between Girart and his nephews Aymeri and Oliver, and between Charlemagne and his nephew Roland. The teasing of the younger heroes by their elders, especially in the latter relationship, where the actions and burgeoning affections of the maiden Aude are involved, presents some of the best *enfances* comedy in the entire genre, and certainly the most cleverly written. The first flowering of Roland's affections for the siblings Aude and Oliver is equally well wrought in dialogue that is both graceful and tongue-in-cheek.

Around such well-known and well-drawn protagonists Bertrand describes only a small circle of honorable and dishonorable minor characters to relieve them or set their actions into relief. Their cameo appearances form brief diversions and simple subplots at regular intervals in the story. Some are traditional anonymities such as unhelpful porters or villainous robbers, while others are famous personalities such as wise Naimes and bitter Ganelon, both acting in type. The original creations of the Duchess-Queen, Count Lanbert of Berry, and Joachim the Jew are convincing embodiments of a woman scorned, an honorable enemy, and an honorable non-Christian, appealing as real people, not just as types. Bertrand's other original characters in *Girart de Vienne*, his hero's father Garin of Monglane, his brothers Milon of Puglia, Renier of Geneva, and Hernaut of Biaulande, and his wife Guibourc, serve two distinct but related narrative functions. First, by aligning Girart ever more closely with the honor and fidelity attached in all the Old French epics to the *geste* of William of Orange (Hernaut, for example, is presented as the father of Aymeri and thus the grandfather of Count William, making Count Girart William's great-uncle), they each become symbols of his moral justification. Second, they serve the narrative purpose of linking the two major epic *gestes*, when Renier of Geneva is introduced as the father of both Oliver and Aude.

Bertrand de Bar's greatest artistic talent, it is generally agreed, lies in his dramatic ability to present clashes of will and feeling with an almost Cornelian intensity. Conflict through direct dialogue is the major narrative technique of the earliest and best *chansons de geste*. The poet excels in presenting this traditional skill within a more "courtly" framework, through the verbal media of violent quarrels, protests, justifications, arrogant rejoinders, sarcastic insults, and through tender exchanges of pity, friendship, and love. He is also is a skillful practitioner in the presentation and analysis of female emotional states. The scenes in which the Duchess-Queen debates her feelings for Girart and Charlemagne, and in which Aude analyzes her fears for her brother's safety when he must fight her lover, are written with a subtlety rare if not unique in Old

French epic. The heightened importance and participation of female characters in the plot overall are features common to most epics of this era, as are the depiction of supernatural forces and the significance of visions and dreams. Such elements betray the genre's attempt to compete with the more elaborate and sophisticated style of the *roman courtois*, preferred increasingly by the more literate and literary aristocracy.

Other standard features of *roman courtois* composition, which are discernible in this epic and in which it is fair to say that Bertrand is a competent but unexceptional practitioner, are the elaboration of travel sequences and the reflection of courtly lifestyle itself in the detailed description of luxurious objects and in the illustration of correct and incorrect modes of behavior. The versification techniques exhibited in *Girart de Vienne* are likewise of a type and talent common to many other epics in French written towards the end of the twelfth century. The emotive qualities of the oral-based epic formulas, when used in descriptions of battles, knights, and weapons, are still evident in the lengthy and ritualized accounts of duel and warfare. However, the strong dramatic possibilities of the old, short assonating *laisse* or verse-block, where the changing assonance of successive *laisses* can be combined with the syntactic flexibility of the epic formulas to create a build-up of emotion in so-called parallel or similar verses, are virtually lost in these later narrative poems. Here rhyme, of a limited and banal sort at that, replaces assonance and the *laisses* lengthen to become more chapter-like in frequency and function, even as the work progresses.

One small but significant feature of the versification of *Girart de Vienne* in which Bertrand de Bar shows extraordinary skill is in his use of the so-called *vers orphelin*, the short six-syllable unrhyming line which terminates each *laisse*. A common feature of late twelfth-century *chansons de geste*, this stylistic feature is used variously in the present poem to sum up a proceedings, locate an action, highlight an irony, underline a sarcasm, establish a conflict, censure conduct, or praise. Similar *vers orphelins* are often used at the end of consecutive verses to counterpoint actions, establish oppositions, underline hatreds, or consolidate loyalties. Uniquely, Bertrand de Bar uses them to adopt an ironic attitude to some of his characters, to point out to his audience some tragic or comic contrast both unperceived and unperceivable by the protagonists themselves. Most frequently, however, the author openly employs the *vers orphelin* to establish and embellish the basic opposition between King Charlemagne the Frenchman and Duke Girart of Vienne and to manipulate his audience's sympathies for both.

Sources and Influences

Despite the undoubted breadth of invention displayed by Bertrand de Bar in his desire to create a new conception of the character of Girart de Vienne and to present a moral re-evaluation of his legendary relationship with the King of France, it is clear that his poem is a composite work incorporating many elements of earlier epic Girart material preserved in folk-imagination or in actual written chant. The poet himself relates on three occasions (lines 81–89, 107–109, and 6557–64) that his purpose is to reveal only the unknown beginning and ending of an earlier popular tale. That the long section dealing with the actual siege of Vienne owes much to details from traditional sources is confirmed by internal differences, discrepancies, and downright contradictions within the major sections of the poem and between them and later compilations such as the *Karlamagnus Saga* and the *Chronique rimée* (q.v.), which preserve versions much closer to the source poem(s) of *Girart de Vienne*. The events and people crucial to the poet's new purpose dominate the work's first thousand or so lines, and some of them—Garin, Milon, the Duchess-Queen, the kissing of the latter's foot—are completely absent from the "siege section" of the text. Again, in the opening and final stages much emphasis is laid on the fact that Girart is *given* Vienne in fief and that he remains therefore a vassal of his equally bound liege-lord King Charles; yet in the central section of the poem several characters, including Girart himself, maintain that Vienne is an *allod*, land won from the Saracens by Girart's ancestor Beuvon "the bearded," and which Girart therefore rules independently and by hereditary right. It is interesting also that Roland and Oliver appear only in this second, less original part. Van Emden has in fact suggested that their famous duel and reconciliation are patterned on a similar confrontation between Count Oliver and the pagan Fierabras highlighted in the popular *chanson de geste* bearing the latter's name, which was written around the year 1170. Two further significant narrative details of *Girart de Vienne* that can be found in the earlier Old French epic called *Girart de Roussillon* are the loss to the hero of a promised bride and a decisive battle halted by divine intervention. The episodes of the quintain, the capture of the courtly Lanbert de Berry, and Oliver's embassy to King Charles, have each been identified as borrowings from an earlier poem (now lost) transmitted to us through the record of the Norwegian saga.

In all later extant *chansons de geste* which feature, to a greater or lesser extent, the imposing personage of Girart de Vienne—most notably the stirring *Chanson d'Aspremont* (c. 1190), the mid-thirteenth century

Auberi le Bourgignon, and the expansive Franco-Italian epic called *L'Entree d'Espagne*, the duke is represented as the disloyal, arrogant baron of the source poem(s). A similar view of him is taken by the historical compilation of Jean d'Outremeuse (d. 1400) called the *Myreur des Histors*, where Girart de Vienne, Girart de Fraite, and Girart de Roussillon are considered to be three different people, and by the Italian Renaissance work called the *Viaggio di Carlo Magno in Ispagna*. However, several of Bertrand de Bar's narrative innovations in *Girart de Vienne* reappear also in these and other works of the epic genre. For example, the *Chanson d'Aspremont* makes mention of four brothers called Hernaut, Milon, Renier, and "Girardet le menor," all sibling names originating in the present poem. The epics called *La Chevalerie Ogier*, *Renaud de Montauban*, *Les Narbonnais*, *Anseis de Cartage*, and *Le Moniage Guillaume* (the so-called second version) likewise name one or more of the brothers given to Girart by Bertrand de Bar. The several manuscripts preserving late twelfth-century rhyming versions of the *Chanson de Roland* not only make much greater allusion to the figure of Girart de Vienne himself but also to certain relationships of his which are established only in Bertrand's work, e.g., his guardianship of the maiden Aude, she being his niece, and his particular affection for his brother Hernaut de Biaulande.

The continuing popularity of Bertrand's *Girart de Vienne* both in France and further afield is attested by the considerable number of prose adaptations which have survived either in fragments (e.g., a Dutch version of the thirteenth century) or in full (e.g., the fourteenth-century Arsenal 3351 manuscript, the quasihistorical *Croniques et conquestes de Charlemaine* by David Aubert, completed in 1458 and later revised at the behest of Philippe the Good of Burgundy, and the several *Guerin de Montglave* incunabula of the fifteenth, sixteenth, and seventeenth centuries). The legend of Girart de Vienne, like that of Roland himself, enjoyed a revival among nineteenth-century poets of the Romantic school. In his 1811 edition of *Altfranzösische Gedichte* the German scholar and poet Ludwig Uhland faithfully and elegantly translates from *Girart de Vienne* the first meeting of Count Roland and Aude. In the section called *Le Mariage de Roland* of his own epic cycle *La Légende des Siècles,* first published in 1859, Victor Hugo recreates the celebrated duel between Oliver and Roland in lines very similar to those of Bertrand de Bar.

The contemporary and lasting influence upon the whole *chanson de geste* genre of Bertrand de Bar's inventive genius and artistic achievement as witnessed in *Girart de Vienne* both were and remain immense. His poem stands at the crossroads of Old French epic writing, interrelating with skill, humor, and grace the legendary protagonists of the three major heroic song cycles (*gestes*) of its time, its prologue introducing a narrative cohesion respected by all subsequent poets and scholars of the genre.

Editorial Policy for this Translation

This translation is based on the edition of Wolfgang Van Emden published by the *Société des Anciens Textes Français* in 1972 from the thirteenth-century copy held in the library of the British Museum in London. It is the only complete copy of the poem extant that is written in one scribal hand. I have almost always followed Van Emden's readings of corrupt or variant lines and am also indebted to his thorough analysis of the poem. My translation follows his division of the poem into four parts, which are discernible but not distinguished in the original: *The Youth of Girart, Hostilities Begin, The Siege of Vienne*, and *The Reconciliation*.

In this translation I have tried to preserve most of the formal properties of the original text. The *chansons de geste* are oral-based poems and the formal powers of such verse (the incantatory effect of formulaic diction, the affective qualities of assonance and rhyme) need to be recreated in verse and read aloud by the modern reader if something of the fine and full effects of this art form are to be appreciated. Like most *chansons de geste, Girart de Vienne* is written in ten-syllabled lines, grouped together in stanzas (known as *laisses*) of irregular length. The final syllables of all the lines in one Old French epic *laisse* were originally assonanced together, but in later poems such as *Girart de Vienne* they are rhymed. This full rhyme, which is easy to achieve in French, is impossible to copy in English and so I have used the traditional assonance patterning. The assonance (or rhyme) changes with each *laisse* and is commonly masculine but occasionally feminine. A feminine ending is one in which the stressed syllable that carries the assonance is followed by an unaccented *e* (*baronnie, folie*); a masculine ending is one in which it is not so followed (baron, donjon). This additional unstressed syllable does not count in the scansion of the line. Thus, in the translation not only do words like *brave* and *jail* assonate, but so do *barons* and *madness*. The line itself is strictly decasyllabic with strong internal accent. There is a break in the line after the fourth syllable (or occasionally after the sixth), and the final syllable before the caesura may once again be either masculine or feminine and may vary from line to line. The heavy end-stopping of the lines of the earliest epics is much less evident in a late twelfth-century poem like *Girart de Vienne*, and in the interests of fluency I have created even more run-on lines.

My thanks go, as always, to my wife Sue, for her patient word-processing of my typescript, and again to my friend Gary Heap for his collaboration on the map.

Select Bibliography

1. Editions

Tarbé, Prosper. *Le Roman de Girard de Viane*. Reims, 1850.

Van Emden, Wolfgang. *Girart de Vienne*. Paris: Société des Anciens Textes Français, 1977.

Yeandle, Frederic G. *Girart de Vienne*. New York: Columbia University Press, 1930.

2. Secondary Texts

Becker, Philipp August. *Das Werden der Wilhelm- und der Aimerigeste*. Leipzig, 1939.

Bédier, Joseph. *Les Légendes épiques*. Paris: Champion, 1908–13; rpt. 1914–21. 1:25–29; 2:3–95.

Benton, John F. "The Court of Champagne under Henry the Liberal and Countess Marie." Ph.D. dissertation, Princeton University, 1959 (University Microfilms, Inc., Ann Arbor, Michigan, 1967).

Beretta, Carlo. "I *Narbonnais* e il *Charroi de Nîmes* (e altre filigrane guglielmine) nella prima parte del *Girart de Vienne* di Bertrand de Bar-sur-Aube." *Medioevo romanzo* 15 (1990): 235–57.

Cirlot, Victoria. "El orden de la palabra y la idea de linaje en *Girart de Vienne*." *Au Carrefour des routes d'Europe, la chanson de geste ...*, 351–65. Aix-en-Provence: Société Rencevals, 1987.

De Riquer, Martin. *Les Chansons de geste françaises*. trans. I.-M. Cluzel. 2nd ed., 161–66, 260–66. Paris: Nizet, 1957.

Elliott, Alison Goddard. "The Double Genesis of *Girart de Vienne*." *Olifant* 8 (1980/81): 130–60.

Frappier, Jean. *Les Chansons de geste du cycle de Guillaume d'Orange*. 2 vols. Paris: SEDES, 1955–65.

Gautier, Léon. *Les Epopées françaises*, 2nd ed. 3:94–114; 4:171–91, 218–32. Paris: Palmé, 1878–92.

Guidot, Bernard. "L'Empereur Charles dans *Girart de Vienne*." *Marche Romane* 30.3–4 (1980): 127–41.

Holmes, Urban Tigner. *A History of Old French Literature*, 260–61. New York, 1962.

Le Gentil, Pierre. "*Girart de Roussillon*: sens et structure du poème." *Romania* 78 (1957): 328–89, 463–510.

Lichtenstein, Gustav. *Vergleichende Untersuchung über die jüngeren Bearbeitungen der Chanson de Girart de Viane*. Marburg, 1899.

Longnon, A. "Girard de Roussillon dans l'historie." *Revue historique* 8 (1878): 241–79.

Lot, Ferdinand. "La légende de Girart de Roussillon." *Romania* 52 (1926): 257–95.

Louis, René. *De l'histoire à la legende: Girart, comte de Vienne (819–877) et ses fondations monastiques*. Auxerre, 1946.

———. *Girart, comte de Vienne, dans les chansons de geste*. Vol. 1. Auxerre, 1947.

Misrahi, Jean. "Girard de Vienne et la Geste de Guillaume." *Medium Aevum* 4 (1935): 1–15.

Subrenat, Jean. "Vienne. Fief ou alleu? (à propos de *Girart de Vienne*)." *Mélanges Jean Larmat: Regards sur le moyen-âge et la Renaissance*, 309–18. Nice: Les Belles-Lettres, 1982.

———. "Dénominations de l'empereur dans *Girart de Vienne*." *Mélanges René Louis: La Chanson de geste et le mythe carolingien*, 691–702. Saint-père-sous-Vézelay, 1982.

Tyssens, Madeleine. *La Geste de Guillaume d'Orange dans les manuscrits cycliques*. Paris: Belles Lettres, 1967.

Van Emden, Wolfgang G. "Hypothèse sur une explication historique du remaniement de *Girart de Vienne* par Bertrand de Bar-sur-Aube." *Actes du IV Congrès international de la Société Rencevals*, 63–70. Heidelberg, 1969.

———. "*Girart de Vienne*: problèmes de composition et la datation." *Cahiers de Civilisation Médiévale* 13 (1970): 281–90.

———. "*Girart de Vienne* devant les ordinateurs." *Mélanges René Louis: La Chanson de geste et le mythe carolingien*, 663–90. Saint-père-sous-Vézelay, 1982.

———. "*Girart de Vienne*, Epic or Romance?" *Olifant* 10.4 (1984/85): 147–60.

The Geography of Girart de Vienne

Laon

Senlis
St. Denis   *Marne*   Reims

NORMANDY

Paris   *Seine*   CHAMPAGNE

Bar-sur-Aube

BRITTANY

Sens

Orléans   Châtillon   *Saône*

Loire

Dijon   Beaune

Bourges   BURGUNDY

Cluny   Chalon

Mâcon   Geneva

Neuville
Lyon
Vienne

Gironde

AUVERGNE

Genèvre

Rhône

Toulouse

GASCONY   Montpellier

Roncevaux   Narbonne

Part One:
The Youth of Girart

1

Lords, will you hear a worthy tale I'll tell,
Of lofty theme and deeds of great prowess?
A better one could not be heard or said;
My song is not of pride or foolishness,
Neither of treason nor of deceitfulness,   5
But of a breed whom may Lord Jesus bless,
As fierce as any who ever yet drew breath;
At St. Denis, in the main abbey there,
We find it written, don't doubt of this one shred,
Inside a book, a very ancient text,   10
That in proud France there only were three *gestes* —
I do not think that any will object;
The best one tells of the kings of the French,
And after that the one held rightly next
Tells of Doon of hoary beard and head,   15
Lord of Maience and very brave himself;
Those of his line were fierce and fearless men
Who could have ruled the whole of the French realm
And been the first in chivalry and wealth,
If pride and envy had not ruled all of them;   20
Of this same line wherein such evil bred
Was Ganelon, who by his treason set
Almighty France to grief and such distress:
Whose treachery unbound sent to their deaths
On Spanish soil among the Saracens   25
    The Peers Twelve of France.

2

In many a song, my lords, you've heard the tale
Of how the line of Ganelon contained
High knights untold of bearing bold and brave,
Fearless and fierce, of great renown and fame;   30
They could have held all France beneath their sway,
If pride and sin had not held them enslaved;
But pride it is, don't doubt of this one grain,
Which has brought low so many of high estate:
As were those angels, the well-known truth we say,   35
Who by their arrogance were cast away
From Heaven's hall and down into Hell's jail,
Where evermore they shall know grief and pain;
Through the great pride and folly of their ways
They lost their place in Heaven's blest domain;   40
And Ganelon's kinsmen were just as they,
Who could have been so rich and so well-famed,
If pride and sin had not flowed in their veins;
Of this same line the second *geste* was made,
    Who never did but evil.   45

3

The third *geste* which was praised in times of yore
Was Garin of Monglane's, the fierce-faced lord;
And to his line, this I can witness for,
There never was a cur or coward born,
No lying villain or traitor among them all;   50
They were, indeed, bold knights and wise in thought
And very brave and noble warriors,
Who never harmed a King of France's cause;
They strove rather to aid their rightful lord
And to increase his honor at every point;   55
The Christian faith they did much to exalt
And to confound the Pagans and their law;
Four sons were born of fierce-faced Garin's loins,
And braver knights than these lived not before;
In one whole day I never could record   60
The sum of the great merits of all these four;
The first-born son, I tell you nothing false,

Was the fierce-faced Lord Hernaut of Biaulande;
The second son, as I have been assured,
Was Miles of Puglia, who won such laud; 65
Count Renier of Geneva was the third-born,
And Lord Girart the warrior was the fourth;
No man could plead a case for finer lords:
They never earned reproach for any fault;
Yet ere these four were raised to knighthood's call, 70
While they were all still youths and raw-limbed boys,
Misfortune struck their father with great force:
For Sinagon, a hostile heathen Moor,
Whose hand controlled all Alexandria,
Came to Monglane to conquer it in war 75
And scorch with fire and pillage and destroy;
Outside its gates they held naught worth a coin,
Unless they fought for it with steel and sword;
May He help them, Who judges each and all,
    Now this great war's upon them. 80

4

Often enough you've heard the stories told
Of Duke Girart, brave Vienne's lord of old,
And Ermenjart and Count Aymeri both;
But all the bards who've served you leave unknown
The best there is to tell about all those; 85
For they don't know the story I'll disclose:
The origin from which the *chanson* flows —
Who Girart was and his father also;
But I shall tell, who know the truth alone;
The lord Garin, of whom you have been told, 90
Fathered four sons who all were very bold;
As knights there were none better to behold;
Yet ere their arms or armor were bestowed,
Or they were given wealth or land to own,
Great poverty drove all of them from home, 95
As you shall hear as my story unfolds:
Maytime it was, with warmth and peace aglow,
With the grass green and flowers on the rose;
In the fine, strong-walled town of Bar-sur-Aube,

Bertrand sat down within a budding grove,   100
A noble clerk, this story to compose;
When leaving church, one Thursday, he approached
A pilgrim there, a hale and hearty soul,
Who'd prayed in praise before St. James' bones;
Returning home through St. Peter's in Rome,   105
This man it was who told Bertrand the whole
Of all he'd heard and learnt upon the road
About the lord Girart and his great woes,
  Before he gained Vienne.

5

One Eastertime, which is a joyous feast   110
For men on earth at the Lord God's decree,
And fills the hearts of all with valiant cheer,
Old Lord Garin of hoary head and beard
Was at Monglane, his strong and wealthy seat,
With his fine wife, whom he held very dear,   115
And his four sons of mighty merit each,
Strong and lithe-limbed and very brave indeed;
Yet his content was robbed by this one grief:
Between them all they had not one bread-piece,
No wine decanted nor any salted meat;   120
Three cakes they had and two peacocks to eat
Within their hall of vaulted walls and steep;
Of these their cook and his crew made a meal;
In their whole town they owned nothing but these,
And one Syrian mule and one war-steed   125
And three stout shields and three well-burnished spears;
No other wealth remained nor property;
Garin sees this and, sick at heart, he grieves
And groans aloud and bitterly he weeps;
The tears fall down upon his hoary beard;   130
Hernaut sees this and the blood burns his cheeks;
He cannot help but speak out, firm and fierce:
"Father, for Jesu's sake, what ails you here?
I see you weep, which seems madness to me;
Don't hide it, sire, tell me why you weep tears!   135
By St. Elijah's bones, if you won't speak,

All of my life I'll have no joy or peace,
    For I would deem it treason."

6

"Father, fine lord," noble Hernaut implores:
"So help me God, the giver of our laws,   140
I see you weep and I fret at the cause;
Don't hide it, sire, or I shall be distraught;
My heart will break in three for grief, I'm sure."
"Son," says the father, "then I shall tell you all;
So help me God, Who is our sovereign Lord,   145
It is for you that I am so forlorn;
When I see you in clothes so wan and worn,
You seem to me to be a townsman's boy,
Of lowly rank and means and manner small;
Son, do you think my heart should not be sore,   150
Despite all I have done, to see you poor?
All this the lord King Sinagon has caused,
Who has destroyed our manors and our forts
And held us back from all our lands by force,
So we may take nothing worth two Mans coins;   155
Our food supplies are now the worst of all;
We have nothing for two or three days more,
    And for my life I'm fearful."

7

"Father, fine lord," Hernaut the wise entreats:
"To grieve so much is a great shame indeed;   160
There's none on earth, if he persists in grief,
Whom his own kin will not hold still more cheap;
And what is more, I'll tell you how I feel:
So help me God, the man who always grieves
At present woes and speaks of future ease,   165
Will not survive as far as St. John's feast;
No fort or city wall withstands his fear,
Nor any towns that are worth twopence each;
No vair, no gray or ermine cloaks he'll keep;
The faithless Jews in this way met defeat   170

Upon Abilant's sands in Egypt's heat,
Where our Lord God had looked after their needs
For a long time with sweet manna to eat;
But they got nothing when they lost their belief,
Instead they lost His helping hand, and He   175
Was right to fail them, since they all disbelieved;
And so it is with wicked folk and weak,
Who do not love Lord God or heed His creed
To save themselves or to increase their weal;
And it is Eastertime, a joyous feast,   180
When the high-born and humble make good cheer;
Therefore, with happy heart give us our meal,
For you know not what you may give in brief."
"Son," says his sire, "you're very wise indeed;
An Archbishop could not so well have preached!   185
God strike me down, if any more I'll weep!"
They ask for water and then they take their seats —
Although in truth they have not much to eat;
When all is gone, the sons make haste to leave;
Hernaut mounts horse, the wisest one of these,   190
The other three on foot race merrily;
They draw their bows with arrows sharp and keen,
For none of them have knighthood's garb and gear;
Out of the gate they race immediately;
Before those walls the Rhône runs noisily,   195
A wondrous flow that is both wide and deep
And brings barges and boats right to their feet;
Without Sinagon's war, the Moor Emir,
They would be rich and powerful indeed;
Girart looks at the rising sun and sees,   200
Along the road where they are running free,
Between two hills and by a forest green,
A faithless band of Saracens draws near;
Some twenty mules piled up with wealth they lead,
    Ill-timed from Spain arriving!   205

8

A worthy plan the four of them propose
As they observe these mules upon the road;

Girart, the youngest, calls out to Renier so:
"I will not hide my thoughts, brother — behold,
Those sumpter-mules are coming here, I know,   210
All loaded up with silver and pure gold!
Garin, my father, is in great need of those,
He and my lady, with no more food at home;
This day I saw my father's tears o'erflow,
And we henceforth must help him fight his woes;   215
This wealth we'll win and claim it for our own."
And Hernaut says: "Let all of them approach,
For by the Saint that pilgrims seek in Rome,
I will strike down the first one to draw close,
Straight through the chest, with my bow's steel-tipped bolt!"   220
Girart says to Renier: "I hope he won't!
If we, like common boys, use archers' bows,
We shall be held in the lowest reproach;
But if we slay with fists or with a pole,
Our courage and our strength would be well shown;   225
A curse on him who shoots first at his foe;
He is a coward, who dares not fight up close!"
Then Miles speaks up, who is both proud and bold:
"I will not let my thoughts lie undisclosed!
Their leading pair I will take on my own;   230
If I cannot meet and defeat them both,
So help me God, I am not worth a groat!"
And Renier adds: "My lords, if I alone
Cannot defeat three of these Moorish folk,
May I be cursed and may I never hope   235
For food and drink from any noble host!"
"I'll take the rest," says the fierce-faced Hernaut:
"Sir," says Girart, "you'll leave me one, I hope!
If I can meet and beat one on my own,
So help me God, then my renown may grow!"   240
When this is said, those sumpter-mules approach,
Steered from the rear by good-for-nothing rogues;
Hernaut sees them and hails them in these tones:
"You sons of whores, halt there your heathen bones!
You must stop here until you pay our toll!   245
You may not leave till you pay what you owe!
I want the half in silver or in gold

Of all this wealth your sumpters here uphold —
No, I'll not share with you, I'll take the whole!
Leave us the lot, whoever grieves or groans."   250
When they hear this, those heathens' anger glows
And one replies, who makes the fiercest show:
"Curse him who'd give you what you ask, and woe
To any man who dares strike us a blow
Or takes from us the smallest coin we own —   255
He'll have no castle left with standing stones!
And if we had the man himself in hold,
His neck would soon hang helpless in a rope."
Hernaut hears this and in a rage half-choked
He runs at him, his manner brave and bold;   260
Full in the face his left fist strikes the rogue,
Then with his right he strikes him such a blow
That he snaps back his neck and breaks the bone;
Down at his feet he lays the villain low;
His brothers run straightway to join Hernaut,   265
And the first Moor that each meets as he goes
He moves to strike with no more challenge thrown;
They fling them dead, down on the open road;
The youngest lord, Girart, is nothing loth:
He boasts the least, but his deeds speak the most;   270
Down at his feet he lays two villains low;
They slay them all and lay those cowards cold
And then they seize those sumpters with their loads,
Then to their town they drive them with their goads;
Back to Monglane and through its gates they go,   275
Not stopping once before their hall and home;
Garin looks out and gladness fills his soul;
He runs to kiss each son and hold him close,
   Now they are rich and wealthy.

9

Now Garin's court is rich and well supplied   280
With noble coins and all that coin can buy;
They all return, those noble household knights
Who had dispersed about the countryside;
Then, after Easter, when the Wednesday arrives,

Those brothers fair, not wasting any time,   285
Step from the church when Mass is said and signed,
And all of them with one accord decide
That they will leave their famous town behind
To conquer lands, each one, in foreign climes;
The eldest one, Hernaut, of valor high,   290
Calls on Garin, whose beard is tousled white,
And on his wife, the duchess shrewd and wise:
"Father," he says, "hear what I have in mind:
Your home is here among the heathen tribes,
And all around your land is seized and fired;   295
But this your town was so well built betimes
That no assault or siege can harm its might;
Thanks be to God, Who makes the dew and sky,
We have brought you such wealth and such supplies,
Won from those knaves who do not pray to Christ,   300
That for one year your court may live and thrive;
With your consent my three brothers and I
Shall leave to conquer lands in foreign climes."
"In faith, it's true enough, father," says Miles:
"I will not hide my wish and my desire   305
To ride for Rome, and wasting no more time,
I'll pray to holy Peter to bless my life
With land and honor, which I do greatly prize!"
These words he said were true and none were lies —
And blest he went and won Apulia's shire,   310
And the Romagna and Palermo besides,
    Becoming Duke of Sicily.

10

The brothers four brook no delay or let;
They mount their steeds and make no more requests;
To all their friends, in tears, they bid farewell;   315
The noble Duke Garin makes great lament,
As does his wife of face so clear and fresh;
Hernaut sets out, and for Biaulande he heads,
A noble town of much renown and wealth;
When he arrives, he finds his uncle dead,   320
Who was the count who held all of that realm;

Give ear, my lords, may Lord God be your friend,
To what befell the worthy marquis then:
He took a wife who was of high descent,
Born to a duke of power and respect,   325
Who held Marsone in fief, as I know best;
And in her womb Count Aymeri was bred,
Whose noble line outshone all of the rest:
    I sing of its beginning.

11

Neither Renier nor Girart the young boy   330
Ask for a squire or men to serve their cause;
Each one mounts up an ambling mule and forth
On their long road they ride without a pause,
Up many a hill, through many a fearsome gorge,
Through many a wood and many a watercourse;   335
Up to Vienne they ride without a pause,
And there they rest, those valiant young lords;
A rich townsman, brave Hervi he was called,
Lodged them that night by the Rhône river's roar;
And richly too he fed them from his board   340
With venison and wine and mead withal;
After their meal they take their ease outdoors
And view Vienne, that worthy town and fort
With marble walls so very wide and tall;
Girart speaks forth, whose heart is strong and sure: 345
"How fine a town this is, Renier!" he calls:
"I've not seen one so fine since I was born!
This city's sire must be a powerful lord
And rich enough if he owned nothing more!"
Back to their host the sons of Garin walk;   350
Their beds are made and to them they withdraw
And take their rest until the morrow's dawn;
From their good host they take their leave henceforth
And he commends them both to the strong Lord
Born of the Virgin in Bethlehem for all;   355
The two mount up their ambling mules and forth
On their long road they ride without a pause;
I shall not tell of their long journey, lords:

They reach Cluny, arriving as night falls,
And lodge that night with good Abbot Morant,   360
Where he feeds them most nobly from his board;
Whatever dish they wish for he has brought;
The worthy abbot treats them with utmost warmth
And when they've eaten he looks at them once more
And then he asks: "Where have you come from, lords?   365
Whose kin are you? Don't keep me uninformed!
And if you are both squires or serving boys
Who are in quest of a rich lord and court,
Tell me that too, if you wish to of course!"
And Renier says: "My lord, I'll tell you all —   370
To tell a good man lies is foolish talk;
I am a son of worthy Garin's loins,
Lord of Monglane in Gascony the broad;
With Pagan tribes each day he wages war;
Within the town, behind it and before,   375
He's now besieged by Sinagon the Moor;
We ride for France and Charles the Emperor;
If he takes us, we'll serve him and his cause;
One year or two, or indeed three or more,
    We will do service for him."   380

12

Abbot Morant, with goodness in his soul,
Hears Renier speak until his tale is told,
Then he responds with love and friendship close:
"My sons, by God, of high birth are you both,
Of a proud line and noble, knightly folk —   385
Much of their deeds and often I've been told;
But tell me this, which truthfully I'd know:
Have you as yet been dubbed as knights or no?"
"My lord, we've not, through poverty alone;
Dire poverty has made us leave the home   390
Of the dear sire whose blood flows in our own."
On hearing this, the abbot's pity shows;
Straightway he bids his seneschal approach
And says: "My friend, do not delay, but go
And fetch these two a new shirt and new hose;   395

For friendship's sake let both of them be clothed
And clad so that their looks and breeding show;
Where'er they ride they'll earn more honor so."
"My lord, just as you wish," he says and goes;
And he brings back all that he has been told,   400
And both those boys are fresh and finely robed:
"God," says Girart, "majestic Lord of Hosts,
We two are now both rich and wealthy folk!
God and St. Peter, good abbot, bless your soul
For these fine goods which you have loaned us both: 405
And by my faith in God it is a loan,
For if I live I'll pay back all I owe!"
When this is said, beds are prepared for both,
And when night comes they go to their repose
Till morning comes and dawn of day has broke;   410
Then once again they dress in their fresh clothes
And seek their leave and mount their mules to go,
Then they set out upon the metalled road;
Beyond Palatre's ford they pass through Beaune
And then Dijon, the praised stronghold of stone,   415
And after that through Châtillon they go;
Through Burgundy they slacken not nor slow
But ride and ride like vassals true and bold
Right up to Paris, that wondrous town and throne;
They seek the King, but he is not at home —   420
He is at Rheims, this is what they are told,
And so they wait, till their impatience grows
And they leave town and on to Rheims they go;
They find Charles there, the strong King crowned in gold,
So in the town they lodge and seek repose;   425
Lords, you have heard and it's the truth, I know,
That a poor man is held in great reproach;
For one whole week Renier and Girart both
Remain at Rheims but do not once behold
The King at court or eat out of his bowls;   430
So, on a Sunday, as soon as dawn has broke,
Girart gets up and calls to Renier so:
"Tell me your thoughts, good brother, and be not loth!
We have been here for seven days all told
And have not spoken to Charlemagne the bold   435

Nor been received at court or even close,
Nor gained one coin, neither one grain of oats!
If we remain within this town, I know
We shall have nothing left to call our own,
No padded mules, no weapons and no clothes! 440
The living fiend has led us to this woe,
For this whole realm is filled with wretched folk!
It is far better in the land of our home;
Let us return — we've overstayed our hopes."
Renier hears this and in his rage half choked 445
He looks Girart straight in the eye and groans:
"The living fiend has lodged inside your soul!
If I return, as you say I should go,
When we come back to Monglane on the Rhône,
All our rich family will greet us home 450
And ask us where we've journeyed on our road;
And I shall say: 'To Paris and the throne,
And then to Rheims where we found Charles the bold
Abiding there, but did not once behold
The King nor drink nor eat out of his bowls, 455
Nor gain one coin neither one grain of oats!'
Then all my kin will treat me like a dolt,
And we shall be the butt of all their jokes!
I'll go to court, God curse me if I don't,
And claim my dues before this day is old; 460
And by the faith I owe the Lord of Hosts,
If any there is rash enough or bold
To bar my way, he'll pay more than he owed,
    Ere ever I depart there."

13

Both young Girart and his brave brother Renier 465
Go to the court, whomever this distresses,
And pass the gate despite the porter's presence;
They ask for water and sit down at the benches;
There they receive a little bread together
And just one drink, most grudgingly presented; 470
When they see this, great anger fills their senses;
The seneschal arises to address them —

He is attired in a rich cloak of ermine
And in a tunic that has been made to measure:
A new-dubbed knight bestowed them as a present   475
And made the man more arrogant than ever;
A staff of apple-wood his hand holds steady
As he cries out in a loud voice and level:
"Come for your oats, you squires, and when I tell you,
Or by the Cross that pilgrims seek in blessing,   480
If you incur even my slight displeasure,
You'll not receive one grain, by God in Heaven!"
"My lord, give me some oats," Renier requests him:
"Since yesternight my mules have not had any;
So help me God, you may make a grave error   485
If you refuse to give us a good welcome!
If you require our services to help you,
We'll give them willingly, if you'll accept them."
The wretched man sees that they come from elsewhere
And thinks, therefore, that they're not worth a penny;   490
These insults high he hurls at them in menace:
"Get up and go, you sons of whores, you shepherds,
You foreigners, you double-talking Bedouins!
No trotting squire or ribald-looking fellow
Who comes here asking for oats to fill the belly   495
Of any mule or hack or any destrier,
Will get his oats given to him by any —
For such a rogue expects his host to help him
To a good fireside spot and then good bedding!"
He lifts his staff and moves to strike young Renier,   500
And then once more he starts to curse him heavy:
"Son of a whore, you slippery young beggar!
By St. Riquier, you will regret your efforts
To steal out of our stores for your own credit!"
Renier responds, the anger in him welling: 505
"Son of a whore, you double-talking felon,
I'd rather die than leave you unrepentant!"
Like a fierce lord he moves up from the benches,
Seizes the rogue and drags his haughty head down;
He lifts his fist and lands a blow so heavy   510
That his whole jaw it shatters past all mending,
And to the ground it spins him down and fells him;

He drags the rogue, seizing one foot, then sends him
Into one corner of Charlemagne's own shed there:
"Be gone, you villain, and may God damn you ever!   515
You know not how to save oats or to spend them!"
He takes the hod and then he takes to yelling:
"Those who need oats, come forward now and fetch them!
The smallest plea shall earn ten times the measure!
God strike me down, if I demand one penny!"   520
He who has least gains from Girart in plenty —
And their own mules shall surely be well fed too,
For Girart sends one load back to their dwelling;
The serving-men flee from Girart and Renier,
For any who approach them there, attempting   525
To take from them King Charles's grain, regret it!
There are that night some forty battle-destriers
Within the town with no oats in their bellies!
A messenger turns back to Charles and tells him:
"In God's own name, my lord, evil besets us!   530
Down in your barn the squires have slain the seneschal!
Upon the floor he lies of your own shed, Sire!
I think the rogues have broken the man's neck there;
Out of his mouth I saw his life-blood ebbing!
You'll lose our love, if you do not avenge him."   535
When he hears this, the King's anger goes swelling;
He calls Gilemer and Gautier to attend him —
One is the provost, the other is his second:
"Close all the gates, bar each and every exit,
And in the morning search every house and dwelling!   540
There is no squire, however rich the wretch is,
Who'll not pay dear, if he has wrought this treachery!
You will slice off both ears upon this felon,
And pluck his eyes and half his nose you'll sever,
So he dares not again earn my displeasure,   545
Touch me or mine or any of my men here!"
And they reply: "We'll do well all you tell us."
Renier, meanwhile, returns to his own dwelling,
And their two mules eat oats to their contentment;
That night Girart and Renier take their leisure,   550
And ere they sleep, eat figs and dates a-plenty,
    And make merry indeed.

14

Barons, my lords, you've heard often enough:
When a man dies and his lifetime is done,
Folk soon forget all that he did and was;   555
At dawn next day, with the first light of sun,
Both of these lords, so brave and bold, get up;
When they are dressed and shod alike, each one,
Renier calls out and hails his brother thus:
"Girart," he says, "let us go, for God's love,   560
Straight to the court — we've tarried here enough!
Let us find out what's being said and done."
"In God's name, lord," Girart replies at once:
"I fear the fate of that foul seneschal
Whom yesternight in Charles's barn we struck!   565
If he is dead, then we may curse our luck —
Out of his mouth I saw his life-blood run;
We broke his neck and he lay there all stunned!
We shall be blamed and shamed, I fear it much;
We've no friends here who will speak up for us."   570
"Don't fret for him," replies Renier at once:
"The King is served by far too many such!
You can be sure, if he is robbed of one,
      He's rushed by fourteen others."

15

The brave young pair act in a worthy way: 575
They go to court without the least delay;
The Emperor, when he sees the dawn break,
Goes to his church and chapel there to pray;
The Mass is sung by his chaplain Guimer,
And many a lord and peer are in the train   580
Which goes with him to hear the Mass proclaimed;
Outside the church some hundred others wait,
Who all have suits to plead with Charlemagne —
But none of them can further them one pace;
And Renier sees the barons in that place   585
And sees the door shut firmly in their face —
And with his boot he kicks it with such weight
It shakes and shifts and opens up half-way;

The guard sees this and, overwrought with rage,
He lifts his staff and brings it down again   590
On Renier's head and cuts an ugly graze;
Renier feels this and fills with hurt and hate
As the guard next pours scorn on him and blame:
"Son of a whore, you do not know your place!
How did you dare, you foreign-looking knave,   595
To come this near and shake King Charles's gate?
Can you not see around you in this place
These noble lords so worthy to be praised,
Who are all dressed in their bright ermine drapes
And foreign furs of miniver and gray,   600
Who still cannot further their pleas one pace?
And you, did you dare to think that you may —
    Dressed in your shabby mantle?"

16

Renier, the worthy lord, answers him so:
"Son of a whore, you wretched, worthless rogue,   605
May Heaven's King, the Lord God, curse your soul!
The heart's not clad in gray or ermine clothes,
But in the breast where God grants that it grow!
Some have high wealth whose courage is but low,
And some are poor who are both brave and bold,   610
Brave men of limb and noble men of soul!
Now by the Saint whom pilgrims seek in Rome,
I'd rather lose my life, St. Denis knows,
Than not pay back the blow that you are owed!"
Renier is fierce, a valiant friend or foe,   615
And he steps back in wrath and great reproach
And kicks the door with all the rage he knows;
He breaks its boards in half with this great blow
And strikes the guard smack in the face and nose;
It was so strong and so fearsome a stroke   620
That both the eyes from that guard's head it drove;
Down on the ground atop the door he groans,
While over him some ten noblemen go
Who do not ask if he is dead or no;
Out from the church see fierce-faced Charles approach,   625

Who hears the row and the great noise of blows;
The Emperor says: "By St. Denis' bones,
Who has so dared to burst into my home,
Break down my door and lay my porter low?"
Geoffrey of Paris says: "My lord, God's oath,   630
Those two young lords in their gray-hooded cloaks
Forced their way in when they found the door closed!"
Says fierce-faced Charles: "Take both of them in hold!
    We shall bring them to justice."

17

Fierce-visaged Charles is filled with dark dismay;   635
With ringing voice he cries aloud and says:
"Who has dared to do this, by St. Riquier?
Within my hall whose gall has been so great
As to break down my door and then to slay?"
"In Lord God's name, I did this," says Renier: 640
"And do not hide my right to do the same!
God curse the soul of such a wretched knave —
He struck me first with his staff, Charlemagne!
He had put on so arrogant a face,
Puffed up with pride for his smart tunic's sake,   645
That he cared nothing for any Jack or James!
But thanks to God I paid him his true wage —
Down on the ground I've flung him to his grave;
True Emperor, for the true Savior's sake,
I can assure you, in any court of state,   650
Of Emperor, of King or Prince the same,
When a good man comes to present his claim,
He should be met with good and noble grace
And not be greeted with a blow to the face!
For some are poor whose hearts are rich and brave,   655
And some are rich whose hearts are poor and pale;
True Emperor, I tell you true and plain
That it is just, by worthy St. Riquier,
For you to give me leave to state my claim,
To tell you who I am and what I crave,   660
Rather than have me struck or stuck in chains!"
"By St. Riquier, he's right!" the French all say:
    "Fine lord, grant him your pardon!"

18

Our Emperor allows his rage to fall,
When he observes how wisely Renier talks;   665
He sees that both are fine and handsome boys
And asks of them: "Where are you from, young lords?
Whose kin are you? Don't keep me uninformed!"
And Renier says: "My lord, I'll tell you all —
To tell a great man lies is foolish talk;   670
I am a son of worthy Garin's loins,
Lord of Monglane in Gascony the broad;
With Pagan tribes each day he wages war;
Now he's besieged by Sinagon the Moor,
Within his town, behind it and before;   675
To learn the tongue of France we have set forth,
And if it pleases you, within your court
With a good heart we will serve you and yours;
One year or two we'll serve you and your cause,
Then, if you please, a third or fourth or more,   680
So we may win both honor and reward."
Says Charlemagne: "Your words are worthy, boys,
And, in God's faith, you are both nobly born,
Of valiant blood and family brave in war;
Yet at this time I have no wish or cause   685
To lodge you here a long time in my hall;
I'll give you both fresh clothing to be worn
And thirty pounds of silver and pure gold;
Back to your lands you can return with joy
And speak of me with honor and with warmth."   690
Renier hears this and his blood almost boils;
He hails Girart in a fierce, angry voice:
"Go saddle up my ambling mule," he calls:
"And straightaway, fair brother, saddle yours!
I need no money, I am no merchant born!   695
By my own faith in God, Who governs all,
If I owned all the wealth within these walls,
I would not keep even one bezant coin;
My knights and serving-men would have it all,
My priests and monks and others who were poor;   700
None of my line have longed for wealth before
And there's no townsman or trader among them all,

And I'll be none till my last breath is drawn!
This King, I see, refuses the support
And worthy service that we would both have sworn;   705
So we must seek another lord henceforth,
Who will honor us better and heed us more!"
Between themselves the French around them talk:
"By Your worthy command, Father our Lord,
How wise these children are and how well taught!   710
If they could stay at length within this court,
They would outdo the Norman Huidelon
And old Gaydon and Droon of Vincent."
"True Emperor," says German-born Gaudin:
"Retain them, Sire — they are most nobly born,   715
And a great deed of grace you will perform;
Both of these youths have come from far abroad,
And in good faith they offer you their toil
In service of your pleasure and of your law."
The King replies: "Then let them both come forth   720
          And swear to be my liegemen."

19

Both youths proceed in a praiseworthy way;
Before the King they move to kneel and make,
In front of all his knights, their pledge of faith;
Then Charlemagne bids both to rise again   725
And hails those knights who serve him and obey:
"My lords," begins the Emperor fierce-faced:
"First I shall raise Renier to knighthood's rate,
And I shall make Girart my squire this day;
If he serves well, he shall be dubbed the same."   730
"We should well grant this much," the Frenchmen say;
A shirt and hose are brought out to Renier
And silken breeches and shoes from Montpellier;
Across his back a bright ermine they drape
And a silk tunic cut to his size and shape;   735
A noble cloak worth many a coin they place
About the shoulders of valiant Renier;
They go to church to hear the Mass proclaimed,
Which is the custom when a new knight is made:

Ere he's allowed to take up arms in faith,   740
He must hear Mass and pray to God for aid
To bring him honor, success and knightly fame
And the right to win land and rule the same;
Then after Mass they lead Renier away
To dub him knight in Charles's hall of state;   745
The squires bring forth the armor he's to wear:
Some iron leggings, which are much to be praised,
And for his back a hauberk double-chained,
And for his head a green helm golden-laced;
A rich steel sword Charles girds about his waist,   750
Then strikes his neck with the flat of his blade;
He says to him: "Renier, be ever brave!"
"Much thanks, my lord," the worthy warrior says:
"With the Lord's help I shall be so always."
They bring him next a stallion swift of pace   755
And by the left-side stirrup he mounts straightway;
Upon his breast a quartered shield they brace
And in his fist a sturdy spear they lay;
Upon his steed a sudden charge he makes —
Lords, had you seen him use his spurs that day,   760
To speed his horse and turn it and to aim,
And lift his shield and lower it again,
And raise his spear and toss it in the air,
Then you would surely have praised and prized Renier!
He is well praised by all the good lords there,   765
But the malicious ones are filled with hate:
"This is a worthy knight!" the noble say:
"True Emperor," says Renart of Pevier,
A wicked rogue, God send him an ill fate:
"I see ahead the price that you shall pay   770
For granting these two youths too much today!
The time shall come when they shall earn your hate;
Garin, their father, who sent them here I'll wage,
Has never had one meal in peace, they say;
When your own father, Pépin, in marriage,   775
Took worthy Berthe, that most praiseworthy maid,
Garin was still an arrogant young knave;
I saw him sail the seas and lie in wait
For pilgrims' ships, he knew well where they sailed,

And he would steal from monks upon the waves   780
And rob the priests in their churches and naves;
For this he was chased out of France in shame
And forced to flee from all his French estates;
He dared not halt till Gascony's domains;
King Yon gave him a wife within that place   785
And gave to him one quarter of his state,
Which he deeply regretted, when the time came!
This Garin, Sire, whom I accuse and blame,
Murdered my uncle with his tempered steel blade;
Now by the Saint whom pilgrims seek in praise,   790
Since my revenge upon Garin must wait,
His sons shall pay most dearly in his place!
True Emperor, I'll not hide my complaint:
You've never given my son one penny's wage,
Nor given me a palfrey or destrier,   795
Yet we have served you gladly, day after day."
God curse the wretch, our Father true and great!
    Envy shall never perish.

20

When Renier hears the traitor Renart speak,
He's so enraged he almost bursts with grief;   800
With anger flushed his brother's face he sees:
"True Emperor, who is this fat graybeard,
Who by his belly must hail from Lombardy?
He must have had so much salt-pork to eat
He's now as big as a gray mare can be!   805
He's born of Bernart's line, it seems to me,
Who robbed Aymon of his fief Autemere;
He is a traitor, this much his looks reveal!
True Emperor, do justice to my plea:
By the bones of St. Médard, I beg your leave   810
To fight this knave no later than I need;
With this great sword whose blows are full and fierce,
I'll prove the fact against this wicked fiend
That my own father is a fine duke and liege;
If I do not make this old graybeard yield,   815
Then have me burnt or hang me from the beams."

Says young Girart: "Good brother, let this be!
By the soul of St. Leonard, whose faith I keep,
If I thought that the King would not be grieved,
I would have plucked the whiskers off this beast!"   820
While he says this, he seizes Renart's beard
And bares a patch where thick hairs once had been!
In pain and shame the old rogue grinds his teeth,
And the French laugh who look upon this scene,
For they detest the wretch Renart indeed;   825
    A curse upon his kindred!

21

"My lord graybeard," the noble Renier calls:
"Your arrogance would never be the cause
If, in my rage, I left this court henceforth;
Nor would I take my armor or my sword!   830
But by the Cross that all the French support,
I tell you this — you'll earn such a reward
That when I leave you will not thank me for!"
When this is said, this time they leave Renart;
King Charlemagne keeps both young men at court,   835
And whenever a plea or plaint is brought,
Renier decides its right or wrong in law;
He serves the King as a well-skilled knight ought:
He frees all Vermandois from a vile horde
Of thieves and robbers, foul outlaws each and all,   840
Who've held the shire to ransom heretofore;
He sets three traps in one mighty assault
And at a bridge some sixty-three are caught;
And when the well-bred knight captures them all,
He does not lock them up three days or four,   845
He hangs the lot, to end it once for all;
    Which is both right and proper.

22

Sir Renier is a knight both fair and fierce,
And rids the King of his worst enemies;
Within the land of my lord St. Denis   850

No man could travel from Paris to Senlis
And not be cut to pieces in between,
For in Serval there was a nest of thieves
Who lived there in the forest below Senlis;
No traveler alive could pass unseen,   855
They were waylaid and killed or captured each;
Complaints of this reach fierce-faced Charles's ear,
And brave Renier likewise is there to hear;
One hundred knights he takes, all armed with steel,
And hides them there among the forest trees;   860
Then he prepares ten pilgrims in St. Denis
To travel through that part of woodland green;
So through they pass with courage and with zeal
Upon their mules, their garments plain to see,
And, as they go, all chanting cheerfully: 865
The sound is loud, the robbers hear with ease
And from their lair deep in the woods they leap;
With ringing voices those pilgrims shout and scream,
And in great rage Lord Renier springs between
With his one hundred knights of high degree;   870
How fiercely now they fall upon those thieves!
How many times they strike with blade and spear
And slit their throats and leave them there to bleed!
Bad luck for those whose necks escape their steel,
For they're all hung with no hint of reprieve: 875
From branch to branch they swing them on those trees!
In such a way Renier sets the land free,
And fierce-faced Charles is filled with joy indeed;
He holds Renier in a friendship so dear
That he bids him before all France to be   880
    His most trusted advisor.

23

Now at this time of which you hear me speaking,
Charles holds a court which never shall be equalled;
At Pentecost, which is good cause for feasting,
The King convenes all of his knights and liegemen   885
And makes himself much honored at this meeting:
He bids Girart to wait on him when eating

And bids Renier, the highly praised, to be there —
And so they are, with no wish to displease him;
One brings the dishes for Charlemagne to eat from,   890
The other holds the large, bright golden beaker
Of well-spiced wine strained through the sieve in season;
Then, all at once, a messenger appears there;
Into the hall, up all the steps, he reaches,
And in a voice ringing with cheer he greets them: 895
"May God the Lord, Who is the world's Redeemer,
Keep safe King Charles, whose deeds are high and fearsome,
And guard his knights whom at his side I see here!
Barons, my lords, show me, I do beseech you,
Where young Girart from Gascony may be here,   900
He and Renier of whom rumor has reached me
King Charles has made a knight at court to keep him;
I've sought them both each morning and each evening
For so long now that I'm worn out and weary!"
"See, we are here!" says Renier, fair of feature: 905
"Fair brother, friend, why have you come to seek us?
Have you some news of our dear friends to cheer us?"
"Indeed, fair sir, do not doubt what you hear now:
Your brother Miles resides in Apulia,
Where he has now a wife of high demeanor,   910
And two young sons whom everyone loves dearly —
You could not find more handsome, noble creatures!
And Hernaut lives at Biaulande on the seaboard,
Where he has wed a woman of that region
And rules through her all of that land and people;   915
He has a son, and none has seen his equal —
They've called him Aymeri, and, lords, believe me,
If he lives long, he will make that name fearful
And will exalt his line and be a hero;
And you, what news have you of your achievements?   920
What land to rule or honors have you reaped here,
That I may tell your brothers, when next I meet them?"
"Fair brother, friend," says Renier, "you are speaking
Most foolishly, to ask me this, believe me;
You can tell them, for I would not conceal it,   925
That we are here serving brave Charles in fealty;
Girart my brother works in the kitchen keenly

To speed the meals — we cannot make him leave there —
Then all the plates he washes, dries and cleans there;
I clear away the tablecloths and beakers   930
And guard them well so nobody can steal them!
The King looks after us and treats us even
Like two hired hacks put out to graze the greensward;
    Thus do we serve the King."

24

Renier speaks up, whose face with valor shines,   935
He looks straight at the messenger and cries:
"Fair brother, friend, God bless and let you thrive!
Is it then true, and no word of a lie,
That Miles is duke of Puglia the prized?"
"Yes, lord, indeed, by blessèd Mary's child!   940
And he has wed a slender, well-bred wife
And has two sons of noble heart and mind;
And you, my lord, does your hand guard and guide
An ancient town or tower, a land or shire?"
"You question foolishly," Renier replies: 945
"Girart my brother, God bless and let me thrive,
Does not know yet the duties of a knight;
But such a cook you've not seen all your life!
You would not know him now, if he passed by!
I guard the tablecloths — their realm is mine;   950
But by the faith I owe Lord Jesus Christ,
If Charles the King of France the far and wide,
Does not give me a realm to rule by right,
I shall serve him no more in all my life,
    But seek another liege-lord."   955

25

Upon the boards the Emperor's hands move;
To all his men he calls there in the room:
"My lords," he says, "did you hear the rebuke
With which Renier replied in his fierce mood
To this same envoy you see in front of you?   960
The archbishop Guirré told me the truth,

As did Renart, the worthy well-famed duke
Of Pevier, whose heart is brave and true:
Whatever grace I granted to these two,
They never would be grateful for what I do; 965
I've heard it said, and now I have the proof,
That when a thief is rescued from the noose,
He'll rob the lord who's saved him from his doom!
From their low state I have rescued these youths
And now, for thanks, it seems I earn abuse! 970
    Their line is far too lowly."

26

When Renier hears the Emperor's fierce speech,
With utmost rage the blood burns in his cheeks;
He lifts his head so all of them may hear,
And says aloud: "Sire, how have you saved me? 975
What town or territory have we received,
What country have you given us or fief?
You've dubbed me knight, that is the truth indeed,
But I have gained no other thanks or fee
From all this land of yours which I have freed; 980
All Vermandois, that worthy land, was seized
By outlaw bands and in the grip of thieves,
But I rode out and saved the land from these;
I hanged them all, yet gained no thanks or fee;
But by the Saint they seek in Nero's field, 985
If this same day you give no land to me,
Then all the love I have for you shall cease;
At dawn tomorrow, without delay I'll leave
    For Garin of Monglane."

27

The King gives ear to Renier's long complaint 990
And, as he does, his lip curls up with rage;
With hostile heart he hails the youth again:
"Vassal, you chose to be my man," he says:
"And bore my flag in any fight or fray
And won much wealth in mangons and deniers; 995

All that we won was there for you to take;
And many a boast before my knights you made
That you would claim, with or without my say,
Lands in this realm and make them your domains;
French and Burgundians would serve your name,   1000
Frisians and Flemish and German folk the same;
You said this like a traitor and renegade;
Now I command you to show me your good faith:
Like it or not, my rights you will obey!"
Says good Girart: "Much thanks, King Charlemagne;   1005
And, if you please, we shall depart straightway;
With hair-shirts on, unshod, bearing our staves,
With broken breeches we shall leave France today."
"Upon my soul, we'll not!" cries out Renier:
"Girart, you speak like some fool boy or knave!   1010
Let King Charles say all that he will or may!
Since he bids us in court to plead our case,
God damn us if we do not stay and wait
　　To hear his final judgement."

28

Our Emperor is filled with rage and spite,   1015
Hearing the words with which Renier replies;
To all the knights within the court he cries:
"Have you all heard, my lords, barons and knights,
These wretches speak, who were favorites of mine?
Today they have repaid me in evil kind;   1020
They have said things which fill my heart with ire;
Now by the Saint for whom God shows His might,
If they are still seen here in three days time,
I'll have them hung upon a well-branched pine!"
Renier replies: "Why have you done this, Sire?   1025
There was a day which you may call to mind,
When I saw you unhorsed during a fight;
I gave you then my long-maned horse to ride,
While I remained on foot, prepared to die;
But I strove hard with my sword's cutting iron   1030
And won a horse, thanks be to God on high;
Now by the Lord and everlasting Christ,

If this is how my service is misprized,
Men silent now shall loose their tongues and cry,
   Ere we leave the French kingdom."   1035

29

"True Emperor," says bearded Do at this:
"These two young knaves, where do they think this is?
Such scorn for you has poured forth from their lips,
And insults which I am so angry with,
That I, in faith, advise that you do this: 1040
Let forty sous be each one's parting gift,
And two hack steeds, unshod and with a limp;
Of these two rogues let your court thus be quit!"
Renier hears this, almost losing his wits:
"You villainous old fool!" he says to him: 1045
"Remember how I pulled you from a ditch
Which two young ruffians had thrown you in!
The smaller one had dealt you such a hit
With his great staff, which was both stout and big,
That you fell back into the ditch from it;   1050
You never would have climbed out of that pit,
When I grabbed your gray hair and saved your skin!
It grieves my heart that you should hate me still;
But by the Saint they seek on Nero's hill,
Were it not for these knights and for the King,   1055
I'd grab those hairs again upon your chin,
Harder this time than any ever did!"
As he says this, he strides in front of him
And strikes old Do so hard with his square fist
That in his mouth five of his teeth are split;   1060
Down on the ground upon his back he slips;
Now Renier sees all of the court's ill-will:
He looks at Pevier's lord, Renart, who did,
When he was knighted, complain to Charles of him;
The wretched man's a weakly, haggard thing,   1065
With a long beard and whiskers all gray-tinged;
Renier the brave strides up to where he sits
And grasps his beard with both of his great fists;
For fourteen steps he drags the wretch with him,

Who runs and trots, not wanting to one bit!   1070
As Renier leads, their bodies bump and hit
Till he reaches the hearth and throws him in!
His beard is burnt and his whiskers are singed,
And he himself would have been burnt and killed,
When Charlemagne runs up and rescues him,   1075
As do all those assembled there within;
    And they break up the struggle.

30

"Mercy, great King," the noble Girart speaks:
"For love of God, laid on the Cross's beams!
Renier my brother is angry and aggrieved,   1080
But he remains a knight both bold and fierce!
In forty lands there's none better than he;
May Lord God's love, which Longinus received,
Let you, fine Emperor, keep Renier here!
I'll be your man, my own freedom I yield,   1085
And all my life I'll serve you willingly
And never fail you while life is left in me."
Girart kneels down at Charlemagne's feet,
But he's hauled up by his gray-furred pelisse
In Renier's hand, which slaps him on the cheek!   1090
"Away, you wretch!" Renier the bold entreats:
"For by the Saint they search in Rome and seek,
I would rather lose limb or life than be
A purchased slave and nevermore be free;
Our lineage would always be held cheap;   1095
But by the faith I owe my friends and peers,
If Charlemagne, the King of St. Denis,
Does not give me a town nor land in fief,
I'll not serve him as long as I may breathe!
    I shall go to my brother."   1100

31

"True Emperor," says Henri of Orléans,
A knight who is both brave and of good breeding:
"Do you forget what Geoffrey did, the German?

He came to court, insulting and conceited,
And made his boast, with all the French to hear him,   1105
That in Senlis and all the Paris region
Your total wealth was not the least coin's equal!
You had no knight among all those convened there
Within your court, Fleming or German either,
Who would defy this Geoffrey's proud demeanor   1110
In field of fight — but noble Renier, he did!
He armed himself and went straightway to meet him;
Down in the field he sent his war-horse speeding
And struck the rogue with his Viana spear-point;
The German's arms nor armor could redeem him —   1115
From his Norse steed he fell dead and defeated;
You gained from this the land around Orléans,
Half of Le Perche and all Laon's outer reaches;
Give Renier land, lest you are charged with meanness!
If it please you, my lord, give him Geneva!   1120
Its duke is dead these past two months and leaves there
No heir at all, fine Emperor, believe me,
Except a daughter, a courtly-hearted creature;
Let Renier marry her and let him be then
    The liege-lord of that land."   1125

32

Our Emperor acts worthily indeed;
His rage relents a little and he concedes,
When brave Henri reproves him with the deeds,
That Renier has served well with little fee;
Thus he speaks out to all his barons fierce: 1130
"My noble knights of France and Hungary,
Of Normandy and Berry — listen to me!
I know in truth and cannot but agree
That Renier here has helped me in my need;
But he today has sold his service dear   1135
And spoken words which have much angered me;
Yet I desire that we should now make peace:
I give to him Geneva, if you agree."
"This is well done," all of his knights repeat;
The Germans and Bavarians entreat: 1140

"Renier, fine lord, go now and thank your liege!
Approach King Charles and kneel down at his feet!
The gift is great and much to be esteemed."
Renier replies: "My barons, hold your peace!
To clamor thus is wrong and makes you seem   1145
Like common folk who have no food to eat!"
Renier says this to Charles: "Much thanks, my liege;
But take good care, this much I do beseech,
Not to fool me by giving me this fief;
For by the God Who judges all and each,   1150
    You'd very soon regret it!"

33

Renier stands there before King Charlemagne;
The Emperor bestows on him straightway
The right to rule Geneva and its domains;
The Germans and the Frisian lords exclaim: 1155
"Renier, fine lord, for God and His name's sake,
Kneel now before your liege, King Charles the great!"
"Lords, hold your peace!" the noble Renier says:
"You sound like youths when you clamor this way
And make your pleas sound like threats and complaints!   1160
Much thanks, my liege," he says to Charlemagne:
"But take good care that you uphold my claim;
Let knights or barons ride with me all the way
Until I reach this realm and my estates,
And let them all bear charters full and plain   1165
So that our rights are known and are obeyed."
"With the blessing of God," the King proclaims:
"You shall leave here with a fine entourage:
The Archbishop of Besançon, Renier,
Hoel of Nantes and Geoffrey, Anjou's brave   1170
And noble lord, whose beard is white with age,
And seven more of noble lineage."
So while Girart remains with Charlemagne,
Renier departs with no further delay;
Hard as they can they spur their destriers;   1175
I'll not spin out the journey that they make —
They ride so long without a stop or stay

Until they reach Geneva sound and safe;
There Renier takes the fair and noble maid
And marries her without one moment's waste;   1180
In the high hall the marriage-vows are made;
It was this lady of whom I now relate,
Who bore brave Oliver, so fair of face;
He was Roland's companion until that day
They were betrayed by Ganelon the knave,   1185
    In the land of the Spaniards.

34

It was this lady whom I have named, my lords,
Who bore the brave and noble Oliver,
And the fair-visaged maid, the lovely Aude,
Whom Roland was supposed to wed henceforth —   1190
Though he did not, it pleased not God the Lord;
Renier, duke of Geneva upon the shore,
Begins henceforth to arm his land for war:
He builds deep moats and raises mighty walls
And sturdy towers and strong castles and forts;   1195
In all his land there is no peer or lord
Who does not come to him through will or force,
To be his man with faith and pledges sworn:
Those who refuse are flung out of their halls;
King Charles the brave remains in his French court   1200
And with him bides Girart, the worthy boy,
Who is well loved by all the peers and lords
Until the day whose deeds I'll next record: 1202a
King Charlemagne rides out to hunt on horse;
He takes with him his huntsman, who bids forth
His hunting-dogs and hounds upon their course   1205
Within the woods, where they are all employed;
And there they take two stags and one wild boar,
And then load up four sumpters with the spoils;
Towards midday, returning from their sport,
The wind picks up and whips along a storm,   1210
And lightning strikes and it thunders and pours;
Beneath a well-branched oak the King withdraws;
Now see an envoy, who's ridden without pause

From Burgundy with sad news to report;
He sees the King and greets him as he ought: 1215
"God save you, Sire, Who is the King of all!
I have come here to tell you this, my lord:
Burgundy's duke, the brave man, breathes no more —
And the duchess would speak with you, therefore;
Sire, set an hour when she and you may talk."   1220
The King replies: "Then listen to my choice!
Tell the duchess, and let her be assured,
That when the day of St. John's feast shall dawn,
She will find me most certainly at Sens."
The envoy says: "She shall be well informed."   1225
He asks for leave and turns back on his horse;
The Emperor is lost a while in thought
Of the fine duke whom he had loved of yore,
And from his eyes the tears begin to fall;
After a while he stops and weeps no more,   1230
For there is nothing his sorrow can restore;
He lifts his head and he beholds Girart:
And with the arrow his bow would next have drawn
He grants the youth lady and land withal;
The day would come when he would rue the choice!   1235
King Charles returns to court at royal Laon
And clothes Girart in robes richly adorned,
And then has arms and worthy armor brought
And dubs him knight with no delay at all;
For love of him he knights some twenty more   1240
And gives to each new armor and a horse,
The finest found within his kingdom's shores;
Charles gives Girart much honor and much joy —
It soon turned to dishonor and remorse,
    When Charles took back the lady.   1245

35

Now when the feast I told you of is nigh,
Of blessèd John, when Christian joy is high,
Great Charles the Emperor at Sens arrives,
Where the duchess of Burgundy abides
With two archbishops, both standing at her side;   1250

The King sees her and lifts his voice and cries:
"Worthy duchess, be welcome in our sight!"
"Almighty God, our Father, protect you, Sire!"
"Lady," says Charles, "your noble husband's life
Is a great loss for you, his loving wife."   1255
"Lord, I am lost in sorrow," the duchess sighs:
"But there is nothing that sorrowing revives;
I seek another husband, so please you, Sire;
For it is custom since old Moses' time
That wives may wed another, if one should die;   1260
My lord is dead and I need one alive
To rule the laws that my great land requires;
If not, I'll lose too much of what is mine."
"Lady," says Charles, "I know that you are right,
And I have here a lord, a handsome child,   1265
Who is Girart, of noble birth and mind,
Valiant and bold and strong of wit and wise;
Garin of Monglane's son, that doughty knight,
Lord of a city in Gascony the wide."
"My lord," she says, "as the Lord God desires;   1270
I shall accept whatever you decide,
    For I owe you my fealty."

36

King Charles beholds the widow of the duke
And sees her grace, her charms and beauty too:
Her eyes are green, her face is fair of hue,   1275
Her skin is whiter than snow on ice to view;
He says: "By God and the blest Maid, in truth,
In all my realm I've found no woman whom
I ever liked more than the rest hereto;
And yet, this one I find so fair and true   1280
That no one else could match her looks or mood;
Now by the Lord Who makes the sky and dew,
I'll take to wife this widow of the duke's!
Girart shall find another somewhere soon."
And as he wished, that was the way it proved: 1285
And what he gained young Girart had to lose;
What awful war and feuding hence ensued,

Where countless souls bid their bodies adieu!
Charles tarries not but summons to his room
The fair duchess to win his purpose through: 1290
"Lady," he says, "I will not hide my mood;
If it please you and you will not refuse,
Then I shall wed — and my wife shall be you!"
When she hears this, the duchess hardly moves:
"My lord," she says, "you jest, I'm sure you do!   1295
No King should take his own land's vavasour
To be his wife, this is the proven truth;
You should receive a Princess, fit to rule,
Or dowager of highest praise and proof;
Give me Girart, the valiant-visaged youth   1300
And lord to whom I first was introduced;
If I spurn him, then I should earn rebuke;
Fine King, my lord, I will not hide the truth:
    I've no wish to be Queen here."

37

Says Charlemagne: "This is a rash reply,   1305
My lady duchess, and you earn blame thereby!
I will not hide that I think you unwise!
Which is worth more — to falter or to rise
And to exalt the honor of your line?"
"My lord," she says, "do not mock me with gibes!   1310
You can be wed to a most high-born bride,
To a Princess, a duke or baron's child;
I, for my part, should marry with my like;
Give me Girart, whom I have heard much prized
As a well-bred, handsome and brave young knight;   1315
Give him to me and I shall not decline,
For, if I did, I would be blamed with right;
Now, if you please, I beg leave to retire
Back to my lodge to speak with men of mine
And take more counsel on your proposal, Sire,   1320
To be your Queen or brave Sir Girart's wife."
"I grant it willingly," the King replies:
"Much benefit may come from good advice."
So with four counts in consort at her side
The duchess leaves and to her lodge retires;   1325

She bids Girart to come and he contrives
Without delay to do as she desires;
Upon his back he drapes an ermine bright
And a silk cape with an Eastern design;
Like a most worthy knight Girart bestrides   1330
An ambling mule well-saddled for the ride;
A richer saddle it would be hard to find —
One hundred pounds of silver the bridle's price!
Along the street, when he begins to ride,
The townsfolk point him out and each one cries: 1335
"See there Girart, the valiant young knight!
How well they fare who serve a worthy Sire!"
Girart rides on, not wasting any time,
And reaching there, dismounts and starts to climb
The steps to where the worthy duchess bides;   1340
She stands to meet him and greets him fair and fine:
"Most welcome here, noble and valiant knight!
I have asked you to come, so help me Christ,
And come you have and in your debt I lie;
I shall not hide from you the reason why: 1345
I spoke with Charles within his palace high,
Where he urged me to such a thing which I
Would neither then consent with or comply;
Now my own plea, Girart, I will not hide:
If you desire it too, take me to wife!   1350
I am not one for speeches, valiant knight;
I've never heard a long speech yet so wise
That parts of it could not be criticized!"
Girart, without weighing his words, replies:
"My lady fair, what wonders you provide!   1355
I can vouchsafe and truly verify
That the world now begins to lose its mind,
Since ladies ask for husbands in these times!
By all the faith I owe the Saving Christ,
The world shall see two summers live and die   1360
Ere it sees me take you or any bride!
Ask someone else, if someone you can find!
You'll not have me, know that without a lie!"
When she hears this, the duchess almost dies:
    She'd never felt so humbled.   1365

38

Girart departs, in no more mood to be there;
He takes no leave from the duchess nor seeks it,
But leaves her there, her breast with anger heaving;
She cannot eat, she cannot drink that evening
And spends the night all restless and unsleeping   1370
Until next day with the dawnlight appearing,
Whereon she dresses, arrays herself and leaves there
To go to church at the shrine of St. Stephen;
Upon the steps of the high altar kneeling,
She prays to Christ our Savior to redeem her   1375
In Girart's eyes, who has spurned her entreaty:
For she loves him more than the King, her liege-lord;
When she has prayed, she goes back and discreetly
Sends forth a squire to urge Girart to see her;
But Sir Girart disdains to do so fiercely: 1380
For two whole weeks he asks that he not see her;
When she hears this, she almost loses reason
And her thoughts race as she debates her feelings:
With the duke gone, she'll have the King, she reasons,
And so requests that Charles come straight to meet her;   1385
And come he does, not unwillingly either;
When he appears, she greets him very sweetly:
"My lord," she says, "I will tell you quite freely
That I am grateful that you have come to me here;
     It fills me with great joy."   1390

39

King Charlemagne of France the widely famed
Comes willingly into the hall well-paved
Where the duchess of Burgundy awaits;
Now they are both within a private place
The King greets her with a most noble grace,   1395
And she, most wisely, greets him in the same way;
She says: "My lord, hear what I have to say,
For you should know my feelings, Charlemagne!
Now it is true you pressed me yesterday;
But I was not aware then of the state   1400
Of certain things which now have been made plain;

I've been advised, in truth and in good faith,
Concerning the proposal which you have made;
And all my house advises me to obey,
And I agree myself with all they say: 1405
For I would rather be Queen for fifteen days
Of royal France, which is so widely praised,
Than be a duchess for fourteen years again!"
When he hears this, the King's delight is plain
And he calls out to all those in his train: 1410
"My lords, why should I hide it more?" he says:
"This is the lady whom I have heard so praised,
And who shall be my wedded wife, I say!"
"You gave her to me, Sire!" Girart exclaims:
"And all her lands and all of her estates!"   1415
But she replies as one quick with a phrase:
"By all the faith I've borne the Lord always,
I would rather be dragged by destriers
Or drowned by waves or burnt to death by flames,
Than any part of me feel your embrace!   1420
For on that day, in truth and in good faith,
When I was given to you by Charlemagne,
I did comply, it was you who complained!
    The shame of that still galls me."

40

Our Emperor acts in a worthy wise   1425
As by the hand he holds the courtly bride,
And he addresses thus his band of knights:
"Behold this lady of visage fierce and fine!
If you agree, I shall take her to wife."
But Girart says: "My lord and King by right,   1430
You do me wrong, and this I cannot hide:
The other day you said that she was mine,
And mine to rule was all her realm likewise;
But I can't challenge you, who are my Sire."
Charles shows no wish at this to change his mind,   1435
And has the lady brought to a church nearby,
Where Renier the Archbishop weds them in Christ;
The wedding-feast fills up the palace high,

And all that day they pass a joyous time;
I will not list the sumptuous food supplied,   1440
There was so much it cannot be described;
As evening comes and Charles moves to retire,
Two Archbishops there bless the nuptial night
And the King's men in this request unite:
"True Emperor, by the Lord God on High,   1445
The noble knight Girart is filled with spite;
Give him a land and fief to rule and guide
So that no man henceforth slanders or slights
Your name and honor for misprizing your knights."
"I shall most willingly," the King replies: 1450
"For love of you, whose embassy I prize,
And for Girart, whom I do prize alike,
I give to him Vienne and all its shire;
Its walls are high, its moat is deep and wide,
And the town rich and much to be admired;   1455
He'll have his fill of food and drink for life;
Against his foes he will be well supplied —
But he must help me, if the need should arise."
All the Bavarian lords and Germans cry:
"Go to his feet, Girart, you worthy knight;   1460
The gift is great — your thanks should be in kind."
"In God's name, willingly," Girart replies;
For Charles's sake, who to his bed retires,
His manservants turf down the hallway's fire;
Now Girart comes before the King's bedside   1465
And kneels to kiss the foot of Charles, his Sire;
But the duchess, in her malicious pride,
Puts forth her foot, on which his kiss alights:
His flesh against her flesh, lords, what a crime,
As if the Devil had got into her mind!   1470
If good Girart had known of her design,
He would rather have struck her with a great knife
Than deigned his lips to touch her on that night!
God! What a war this kiss shall cause in time,
And how many fine knights are doomed to die!   1475
    It should be her to perish!

41

Girart the duke, the valiant-visaged lord,
Now rules Vienne, a city famed and sure,
Given to him by Charles the Emperor;
But Duke Girart has no idea at all   1480
Of the deceit of the evening before,
Which the duchess in her raging remorse
Did to his shame in her room in the hall;
But how dearly that deed will cost henceforth!
How many souls from bodies will be shorn —   1485
Though she herself should be the first forlorn!
But now the King has married her, she's called
The Queen of France from the south to the north;
The morning comes, and with the light of dawn
Girart the duke would tarry there no more,   1490
And after Mass he takes leave of the court;
The King fits him with a fine household force
Which he will take to his new land and fort,
And a great wealth he takes in kind and coin
Which Charlemagne has won in lands abroad;   1495
They ride so far with every day that dawns
Until they come to Cluny one nightfall
And to the abbey so richly built of yore,
        Where they will lodge that evening.

42

Within the abbey walls they lodge that night: 1500
"Abbot, do you know me?" Girart inquires:
"No friend, in truth," the good abbot replies:
"I have never seen you in all my life."
"In God's name, yes you have!" young Girart cries:
"Renier the praised, my own brother, and I   1505
Some fifteen years ago came traveling by,
And you showed us great kindness at the time:
You gave us robes for our shabby attire
And I have not forgotten your charity!
Now I shall give to you a gift of mine: 1510
One hundred marks of silver and silks sewn fine,
Which will serve you and your abbey in kind."

When he hears this, the abbot's thanks are high,
And all the monks bow down with thanks likewise;
Girart departs next day at dawn's first light,   1515
And straight towards Vienne his party rides;
His envoy spurs in haste till he arrives
At Vienne town and gallops straight inside;
Throughout the town he spreads the news and cries
That their new lord is coming, a valiant knight   1520
To whom great Charles has granted all their shire —
And they should go to show him their delight,
Without delay, as their liege-lord by right;
And when they hear him speak, they waste no time
But in a crowd they move to meet their Sire;   1525
Even the bishop, the holy clerks and friars
Move out to meet Girart in loyal lines;
They welcome him with noble pomp and guide
Him through the gates, rejoicing all the while;
They sing a Mass at St. Maurice's shrine,   1530
Then all the folk of all that fief unite,
Both high and low, with true and willing minds
To pledge him faith and homage all their lives;
Then all their lords with great rejoicing climb
  The steps to Vienne palace.   1535

Part Two:
Hostilities Begin

43

Girart resides in Vienne's hall of state;
He is well loved by all in his domains,
And that same year, after Ascension Day,
Upon the feast of John the blessèd Saint,
He takes a wife of high repute and race —   1540
King Othon's sister, and Guibourc is her name;
It was this lady, of whom I now relate,
Who bore Beuvon and then Savariez;
There came a day, when in his Pagan jail
King Achatanz held both of them in chains;   1545
But now Girart bides in his hall and waits
High at a window most beautifully made;
He scans the road which leads through a deep dale
Between two hills to Lyon on its way,
And sees a youth approaching as fast he may;   1550
He travels with two others in his train,
Each on a mule of Aragon arrayed;
Their saddle-bows of gold are all engraved
With painted flowers and animals ornate,
And all the studs are gold along their reins;   1555
Dismounting on the blocks in the hall's shade,
They leave their mules in worthy Guion's care,
Who is the porter of Lord Girart the brave;
These youths stride up the palace steps in haste:
Lords, one of them is Aymeri by name,   1560
And he comes first into the hall of state;
Girart sees him and his whole face turns pale:
    The lad's so like a kinsman!

44

Young Aymeri strides up the staircase boards
Into the hall which is both high and broad;   1565
Upon his wrist he bears a sparrow-hawk
As white as the auburnum's leaf and more;
Girart the duke acts in his honor's cause:
When he beholds proud Aymeri stride forth,
He calls his knights and tells them each and all: 1570
"My lords," he says, "pray silence all your talk!
For I see here a young and carefree lord
Whose eyes are only for his fist's sparrow-hawk!
Let none of you, soldier or squire, step forth
And dare to speak one word with him before   1575
I first have said my own words to the boy."
His men reply: "We will obey, my lord."
And so the youth strides up into the hall
And starts to speak in a loud, ringing voice:
"May the Lord God, Who judges each and all,   1580
Protect and bless this home of valiant lords!
Where is Girart, brave lord and warrior,
The noble duke whose fame I have been taught?"
Soldier nor knight makes the least sound or noise,
But stoop their heads and gaze straight at the floor!   1585
When he sees this, the young lord fills with gall
And in a rage he starts to curse them all:
"You worthless rogues, you boors, you sons of whores!
A curse on him by whom you have been taught,
If I alone can fright you with my voice!   1590
I've fifteen pounds of gold I can employ
To pay for lodgings within this town of yours;
And food and drink a-plenty I can afford
Despite you all, you weak and wicked horde!
You all display the manners of a boor: 1595
You have no heart unless your gut is gorged!"
Girart hears this and with a laugh he roars:
"Who are you, brother?" the brave man asks the boy:
"These nobles here have heard a matter brought
Of high concern and they must judge the cause;   1600
Your strong-willed words weigh little on their thoughts!
Now speak up lad, then seek lodgings and board,

Then come back here and dine with us at court;
And ply your trade, if you are a jongleur!
And if you want to sell that hawk of yours,   1605
Then I will see you get one denier coin!"
Then Girart calls his head-treasurer forth:
"Put on that perch this young man's sparrow-hawk;
He has no skill in holding it at all."
When Aymeri hears this, in rage he roars: 1610
"You worthless rogue, you boor's son of a whore!
No serving-man of birth or mind so poor
Ever served my father, fierce-faced Hernaut, before!
I cannot bring myself in word or thought
To call you uncle — I shall return therefore   1615
     To Hernaut of Biaulande."

45

When Girart hears the youngster's lips disclose
That he's his nephew, he feels a joy unknown;
Yet he would hear him speak fully provoked,
For he suspects his mettle, even so: 1620
"Come on," he says, "come on, play us a note!
Are you a jongleur? Sing us a song of old!
I shall give you my ermine fur-lined robe,
And with his gift no lord here will be loth."
The lad hears this and never felt so wroth;   1625
The anger burns his cheeks like flaming coals;
He lifts his voice with rage and hate aglow:
"Now by the Saint in Nero's field at Rome,
Such service as I have been taught to show
I'll surely give to you, like it or no!"   1630
He lifts his hawk, at this, and lets it go
To strike the brow and bridge of Girart's nose;
His mouth and chin are cut and the blood flows
Upon the front of his ermine fur-coat;
Girart cries out: "Take this villain in hold   1635
And let him hang upon the gallows-rope!"
More than three score rush up, as they are told;
Says Aymeri: "Get on your feet, you rogue!
I am the son of the brave knight Hernaut,

Lord of Biaulande, of whiskers white and old,   1640
And nephew of Girart — let this be shown:
I have a letter inside this parchment's folds!"
Girart hears this and, unrestrained, he goes
And grasps the boy — then, lifting him up close,
On mouth and chin seven kisses he bestows: 1645
"Aymeri, nephew, you have a valiant soul,
      And are well like a kinsman."

46

Young Aymeri, both brave and knowing, says:
"Uncle Girart, you showed small wit today,
To hide from me your true self in that way!   1650
For by the Saint in Nero's fields acclaimed,
If at that moment when I was so enraged,
I'd had a stick which my hand could have raised,
I would have struck your head a blow so great
That I'd have split your brains and you'd be slain!   1655
The loss, once gone, could not have been regained!"
Says Lord Girart: "Nephew, it was my aim
To test your worth and your prowess that way!
Now I love you the most of all God's race!
Tell me, my boy, how does my brother fare,   1660
Hernaut the count, whose name has won such fame?"
"In God's name, lord, he is most wise and brave,
A wealthy man in high content and hale,
Fierce-faced and bold and by his friends well praised;
I have come here to see your own estate,   1665
To view your wealth and your own noble sway."
"Son," says Girart, "I am most glad you came;
And I shall knight you before you leave again,
With armor bright and a swift destrier."
"Lord," says the lad, "let your desire prevail!"   1670
And now Girart has his fierce will obeyed
And shows his pride and power through the state,
Constructing towers and barbicans and lakes;
He fortifies Neuville and then he takes
The keys of Lyon town into his care: 1675
His stronghold on the Rhône the town became;

And so he thinks that he and his are safe:
And yet, before six months have spent their days,
The duke shall have much warfare and much pain,
Enough to fill his heart brimful with hate;   1680
All winter through he rests though, as he may
Till Eastertime and summer turns again;
Young Aymeri comes to him then and says:
"My lord, please hear the plea I have to make;
If you agree, to France I will away   1685
To see the King, the mighty Charlemagne;
My father, who is wise, advised the same."
"Nephew, I do approve," Duke Girart says:
"In a high court your honor can but gain;
You could not lodge in any finer place   1690
Than Charles's court, whose honor is so great,
And who has raised us all through his own fame
And through his gifts of lands and great estates."
So Aymeri prepares to leave straightway;
Girart is rich and gives him much to take   1695
In gold and silver and many deniers;
He takes with him two youths in entourage,
Who will attend and serve him in good faith;
Through Burgundy they set out on their way,
These worthy three, and traverse Brie's domain;   1700
From morn till night they neither stop nor stay;
They cross the Marne at Saint-Maur-des Fossés
And see the belfries of Paris tall and great;
At length the three pass through the city gates
And seek the King, but do not find him there: 1705
"The Emperor you seek, bright youths and brave,
Has gone to St. Denis this day to pray."
When they hear this, the three do not delay
But ride along the metalled road again;
Outside Lendit they meet with one Gautier   1710
And Gilebert, who are two powerful knaves,
Who've robbed full many a traveler and slain;
And in their gang there's many a rogue the same:
Some ten of them are with the pair this day;
They see the youths and do not move away;   1715
They pass them by and greet them with 'good day';

But then they say: "We must have lost our brains!
These three young boys are of high birth and name:
The one in front, so well-dressed and arrayed,
Is a young count or prince of some domain;   1720
If we could throw the three of them in jail,
Then we could gain more ransomed deniers
Than four pack-mules upon their backs could take!"
So those ten thieves turn back upon their way
And grasp the steeds those youths ride by their reins,   1725
With firm intent to drag them from the lane;
But Aymeri is in no way afraid;
With ringing voice he calls aloud and says:
"Lords, is this earnestness or some wild play?
Do you want money? From our purse you may take   1730
One hundred sous or more in deniers."
Their leader says: "Young fool! Your words are vain!
The three of you will soon be thrown in jail;
For seven months you'll not escape your chains
Till you give us a full two bushels' weight   1735
Of bezant coins and bags of deniers!"
Says Aymeri: "You ask too much, in faith;
We do not have as much coin as you crave;
But by the Saint in Nero's field acclaimed,
If we allow ten thieves to block our way,   1740
In every court we'd earn reproof and shame!"
While Gautier demands and holds the rein,
The noble sword he wears shows at his waist;
See Aymeri withdraw it from its case
And strike the thief who holds him thus detained!   1745
Down to his teeth the sword cuts through his face;
His comrades turn and all try to escape,
But Aymeri pursues them all the same
And both those squires with Aymeri give chase;
Lords, do not think that any got away —   1750
They are all caught, all cut down and all slain!
The three young lords ride on their way again
And come at last to St. Denis that day;
Before the King sits down to dine, they've placed
Their steeds in stables within the town and made   1755
Their way to court to speak with Charlemagne;

When they arrive, the entrees have been laid;
They ask for water and sit down at their plates,
Yet no one speaks one word with them or phrase;
Lord Aymeri is well-born and well-raised   1760
And takes a share of food he sees displayed;
He gives his friends a part of all he takes
And just as much as they desire he shares;
The Frenchmen there, with lowered voices, say:
"This young lord here is high of heart and grace;   1765
He must be born of a proud lord and race;
He will be rich, if he lives to ripe age!"
When plates are cleared and drinking-cups are drained,
The courtiers rise and cloths are cleared away;
Now Aymeri has no wish to delay;   1770
Before the King he kneels straightway and says:
"May God our Lord, Who bore the Cross's pains,
Protect our crowned and strong King Charlemagne,
The noblest Prince in Christendom's domains."
"My friend," says Charles, "may God bless you the same!   1775
Where are you from and where bound, tell me, pray?
And do not hide from us but tell your name!"
"My lord, I am called Aymeri," he says:
    "Hernaut of Biaulande's son."

47

The Queen speaks up: "Here is a fine young fellow!   1780
None fair as this came ever from Auvergne!
Youths full of spite and treasonable wretches
All hail from there, this is the truth I'm telling:
Even Girart, mighty Vienne's protector,
I do not prize the value of one bezant!   1785
Son, who are you? Do not hide or dissemble!"
"I am called Aymeri, lady," he tells her:
"Son of wide-bordered Biaulande's lord, called Hernaut,
And I am brave Girart of Vienne's nephew!
Lady, do not speak ill of him, I beg you;   1790
So help me God, my heart would be too heavy!"
Across the hall a monk hastes with a message
And tells the King: "My lord, good cheer and merry!

Those rogues and thieves, whose evil deeds were many,
Have all been slain, thanks be to God in Heaven!   1795
This very day three noble youngsters met them,
And one so fine whose like I have seen never:
Much like this lad here standing in your presence."
The King hears this and straightaway he questions:
"Was this one you — do not hide or dissemble?"   1800
"In God's name, Sire, it was me, I confess it;
They set on me, this is the truth I'm telling;
In self-defense I slew them and they perished."
The King says this: "And stoutly I'll defend you
Against all those who would seek to condemn you!   1805
    You've done a valiant deed!"

48

Says Charlemagne: "Fine knights of high esteem,
This noble youth is very brave indeed,
Who, without help, has slaughtered ten strong thieves,
Who in our land had done such evil deeds;   1810
Fine, noble youth, do you say truthfully
That you are Hernaut Biaulande's son, the fierce?"
"Yes, Sire, in truth," young Aymeri repeats:
"The noble count makes this appeal through me,
That you should dub me knight, my noble liege;   1815
His love of you forever will increase."
"If you live long enough, a knight you'll be,
And shall bear arms on this day in two weeks!"
The youth replies: "Much thanks for this, my liege;
Farewell until that day I am received."   1820
That evening, ere the daylight disappears,
King Charles returns to Paris, while the Queen
Remains in residence at St. Denis,
And with her bides the valiant Aymeri;
When evening comes and they sit down to eat,   1825
The Queen begins to be more free of speech:
"Listen to me, brave knights well-bred and free,
And I shall tell you what I've never revealed:
My husband died, the duke of Burgundy,
And I was widowed with all my lands to keep;   1830

I came to Charles, the King of St. Denis,
And bade him find another lord for me,
To be my husband — and Sir Girart was he!
I summoned him to ask if he agreed;
To my humiliation, he would not meet,   1835
But asked instead for me to wait two weeks!
I tell you truly, I was struck down with grief;
Then I asked Charles the fierce to come to me,
And he came straightaway and willingly;
Thanks be to God in Paradise the sweet,   1840
Charles married me with his friends' love and leave;
When day was done, after our marriage-feast,
The King was begged by knights of high esteem
To give Girart Vienne and all its fiefs;
The King of St. Denis lay next to me   1845
And Lord Girart came to our bed to kneel
And thank King Charles, his liege, of visage fierce,
And kiss his foot in thanks, or so it seemed:
Before the King's I placed one of my feet
Upon the top of our gray covering-sheet   1850
And made Girart the marquis thus kiss me,
Flesh against flesh, I pledge this faithfully!
No man alive knew of my trickery;
On Girart's pride my vengeance I achieved;
I paid him back for making light of me,   1855
      And took delight to do so!"

49

Young Aymeri, of courage fierce and tall,
Hearing the Queen with pleasure in her voice
So pride herself on the great shame she'd wrought,
Thinks that he'll lose his wits in rage for sure;   1860
He'll eat no more, though all his limbs were shorn,
But leaps straight up in anger and remorse
And starts to speak in a loud, vengeful voice:
"Lady," he says, "by good St. Riquier's corpse,
If you did this of which you have made vaunt,   1865
I will not hide, you acted like a whore!
For brave Girart is a most worthy lord;

I'll die of grief, if my revenge falls short!"
He holds a knife which has a sharp steel point;
Before them all at dinner in the hall   1870
He aims it at the Queen and hurls it forth;
Straight through her breast the dagger would have borne
But she drops to a cushion spread on the floor;
The dagger slams into a wood support;
Fierce Aymeri storms up to where she falls   1875
And would have slain her without a doubt at all,
When he is dragged aside by several lords;
They clutch and claw both at his back and fore
To catch the youth as he flings out the door,
And they go close to capturing the boy;   1880
But Aymeri is in no mood to pause;
He hails his fellow youths and thus he calls:
"My worthy lords, let us return henceforth!
This is an evil land to bide or board;
May God curse me, if I'll stay any more!   1885
      Back to Vienne I'm going."

50

Out of the room young Aymeri has run;
The Frenchmen say: "By God, Father above,
What evil strife comes from a woman's tongue!
My Lady Queen, you have brought us ill-luck!   1890
Why did you speak of what was known to none?
If this sharp knife, which in the beam is stuck,
Had found its mark and you, Queen, had been struck,
Then your vain talk would have been dearly done!"
"My lords," she says, "such terror filled my blood   1895
That I shall not recover for one whole month."
Young Aymeri has lost none of his pluck:
Upon the road he sets his steed at once
Back to Vienne the same way he had come;
From morn till night they keep their journey up   1900
Till they arrive one evening at dusk;
Lord Girart sees him come with joy and love;
Around his neck he holds him in a hug:
"Nephew," he says, "welcome back home to us!

Have you seen France and Charles the Emperor?   1905
Have you gained gifts and a knight's armaments?"
The youth says nothing, his anger is too much;
For a short time he greets or speaks to none,
But then he says aloud and clear enough:
"By God, fine uncle, we three have had ill-luck: 1910
My face shall not be seen in France by such
    As love the Lady Queen there."

51

"By God, fine uncle," says Aymeri the fierce:
"What evil news from France I bring with me;
Your stay at Charles's court was cursed indeed,   1915
For you've been shamed most foully by the Queen,
And all your line shall feel the shame and grief:
When Charlemagne made the duchess his Queen,
That night when Charles and she retired to sleep,
All of his men came to him and appealed   1920
That you should have this land to rule and keep;
To thank King Charles you came on bended knee
To his own bed; but the Queen spitefully
Put forth her foot, and this your kiss received!
The other day she boasted of this deed   1925
Before me and her knights at St. Denis;
I would have slain her with my great knife of steel,
But all her lords forced me to turn and flee."
When he hears this, all Girart's senses reel:
"By St. Maurice," he cries, "whom I hold dear,   1930
If I can call all my fierce barons here,
I'll go to France and fight them till they yield!
I shall not leave one castle in one piece,
No fort or town, no church or monastery!"
Says Aymeri: "By God, Who judges each,   1935
If what you pledge you truly would achieve,
Then take me first to help you in your need;
Renier, my uncle, will aid you with all zeal,
And my father Hernaut likewise is fierce,
And Miles the duke whose valor is esteemed."   1940
"We shall ride to Renier!" Girart decrees,

And straightaway he makes ready to leave;
They bring him arms of gold and silver clear,
And on the road they set out with all speed;
From morn till night they ride until they reach   1945
Geneva town as evening draws near,
And then dismount, at last, from their good steeds;
To see them there fills Renier with good cheer;
He welcomes them to stay most joyfully;
When they arrive in his great hall, they see   1950
A proud young lord whom Renier bids them meet:
"Behold," he says, "fine knights of noble breed,
The courtly son who has been born to me!"
Girart says: "Truly, his look is fierce indeed;
You should praise God in thanks for such as he!   1955
What is his name? Don't hide it or conceal!"
"His name is Oliver," Renier reveals;
Girart replies: "In truth, I'll hold him dear,
    For he looks a fierce warrior."

52

In the paved hall the two brothers abide;   1960
Girart the duke, of features fierce and wise,
Calls on Renier and speaks to him aside;
There he reveals and tells him of the slight
He has received from the Queen and her pride;
Renier hears this and both his cheeks turn white;   1965
He swears to God, Who makes the dew and sky:
"Her villainy shall pay an awful price!
We shall lay waste to France with sword and fire
And lead away in shame great Charles's wife,
If they do not hand her to us betimes;   1970
Then she shall bear our vengeance for her crime;
If this affair were made known now to Miles,
Our noble brother, of features fierce and wise,
He would come here straightway and not think twice;
And Lord Hernaut of valiant heart and mind,   1975
And Lord Garin, our father bearded white;
When all of these have gathered all their knights,
They'd ride in arms up to the Sea of Ice!"

"You speak the truth, brother," Girart replies:
"Without delay send three men who will ride   1980
To seek these counts and bid them from their shires,
    In Vienne to assemble."

53

Between them both, brave Girart and Renier,
They name the time and term and fix the day
When their great hosts, with all the haste they may,   1985
Shall meet before Vienne upon the plain;
Then Girart leaves without the least delay
Together with young Aymeri the brave,
And both return to Vienne in all haste;
Girart is rich and rules a wide domain: 1990
He gathers meat from all of his estates
And slaughters venison and garners grain
For the great armies arriving as arranged;
In his high keep one day Girart awaits;
Towards Lyon he looks and turns his gaze   1995
And sees one thousand knights spurring in haste;
He calls brave Aymeri to see the same:
"Fine nephew mine, heed what I have to say!
I do not know this folk upon the plain,
But I hope they are Moors or Pagan knaves   2000
Or some such folk whom we must fear and face!"
When he hears this, the young lad laughs and says:
"Uncle, I will not hide from you their names:
This is Hernaut of whiskers white with age,
My own dear father, whose life has won such fame: 2005
Consider now where we may lodge his train;
There are more than one thousand, I estimate,
    In service of my father."

54

Girart mounts horse without one moment's pause,
With Aymeri whose valor is his ward;   2010
They leave Vienne by the main street to join
The host that's come from many miles abroad;

Young Aymeri beholds his father's force
And knows straightway the ensign of Biaulande:
He fills with joy, of this you can be sure;   2015
Hernaut appears out of a woodland small;
When he sees him, Girart goads his good horse
Towards his brother and lets the reins both fall;
He reaches him and greets him with great warmth:
"Tell me, fine brother, will you lend your support?"   2020
"I will, by God Who made the sky!" he calls:
"Ill-starred the hour that mighty wrong was wrought,
And by the Queen it shall be dearly bought —
She shall be slain and her name brought to naught!"
While Girart and Hernaut embrace and talk,   2025
See Miles appear, who too has brought his force,
Two thousand strong, to his brother Girart;
He goes to meet and greet him with great joy;
And from another side see surging forth
Renier the duke — he's not delayed at all;   2030
And at his side there's a fine entourage
Of high-born lords and folk less highly born,
But all of them armed and equipped for war;
　　Now Girart's might increases.

55

Straight to Vienne the brother-counts proceed,   2035
Where all are lodged, the mighty and the mean;
While they dismount and start to take their ease,
Behold Garin, the count's father, appear,
Lord of Monglane, of courage high and fierce;
Within his ranks ride seven thousand shields   2040
On long-maned steeds which are weary indeed:
And his men's coats of mail are broke and breached,
Their helmets split and all their bucklers pierced —
They are worn out, for all have fought with zeal
Against the foul and evil Pagan breed;   2045
Thanks be to God, they have dealt them defeat,
But they have borne great loss and injuries;
When these brave men arrive, how joyfully
They welcome them and greet them all and each;

Up to the hall with marble all a-gleam   2050
   Garin Monglane goes striding.

56

Garin the duke the palace steps bestrides
And his sons rush to hug and kiss their sire;
They lead him off to bathe and dress inside,
Where he is clad in cloth most rich and fine;   2055
A rod of apple-wood he holds upright:
From here to Montpellier no man's his like;
When each has dined, all leave the hall that night
Save Garin and his sons, and with that five
Bides Aymeri, the brave and worthy child;   2060
Girart speaks out, of heart and honor high;
Before his brothers and with his father by,
Whom he most dearly loves, he speaks his mind:
"Give ear to me, my noble, well-bred knights;
You have come here to help me with your might,   2065
But you know not, as yet, the reason why;
I served King Charles, the Emperor fierce-avised,
Until one day he went to hunt the hind:
From Burgundy a messenger arrived,
Who came to Charles with sad news from that shire: 2070
The brave and worthy duke himself had died;
Then with his arrow, whose tip was sharpest iron,
Charles gave to me the duchess to be my bride,
And all her land to govern and to guide;
But this same gift was dearly sold in time,   2075
For he himself took the duchess to wife!
That marriage night, when both to bed retired,
King Charles was urged by all his lords and knights
To give to me this town and land entire;
I went to kiss his foot, in thanks, that night,   2080
But his new Queen, in her malicious pride,
Put forth her foot, which took that kiss of mine;
Then she made boast of this, in her proud spite;
Young Aymeri, whose heart is fierce and high,
Heard of her trick and so did many knights;   2085
Without revenge my rage will end my life,
   The shame of it's so heavy."

57

Garin the old now to his feet gets up;
As he beholds his sons he tells them thus:
"My lords, you are, each one of you, my sons;   2090
Both you, Hernaut the wise, and you, Milon,
Went off to win your fiefs with blade and blood;
To noble France Renier went to become
A serving knight, and Girart did as much,
Like shepherds guarding sheep, the two of them;   2095
I tell you this: if Charles has wit enough
To swear to you in front of everyone,
That he knew not and it pleases him none
To learn of this great shame with which you're stung,
Then he shall not deserve hatred of us;   2100
It is not long, so help me God above,
That I clashed arms with Emir Sinagon;
I was besieged by hordes of Saracens
Within my town, behind it and in front;
I do believe if I had peace for once,   2105
I would be struck by sickness within a month,
Or leprosy or some great plague or such!
But when I see the whinnying war-steeds plunge
With worthy knights into a battle's crush,
And see their spears and cutting blades well struck,   2110
There is nothing on earth I love so much!
Yet, if the Emperor has wit enough
To swear to you in front of everyone
That he knew nothing of this great insult done,
He shall not feel the hate and wrath of us;   2115
But should he not, my worthy knights and sons,
Then awful war and heavy shall result,
        And we shall overrun him!"

58

When Aymeri hears his grandfather speaking,
He seeks Girart and speaks out, when he sees him: 2120
"Uncle, have your ears heard this old man's preaching
And proud account of the great fights he's been in?
You would be called a fool and with good reason,

To lead him forth to more, if he's so weary!"
Garin hears this and thinks his wits will leave him!   2125
He holds a rod, to grace his age and please him,
And now, in rage, he raises it to beat him;
But the youth turns and Garin cannot reach him:
"Son of a whore," shouts old Garin the fearsome:
"No man can well amend his plans on hearing   2130
A willful youth whose words are overweening,
And not be blamed by all for his own weakness!
   We'll pay no heed to you!"

59

Hernaut the count, a man of boldest vigor,
Leaps to his feet and shows a valiant visage;   2135
He speaks aloud and all his brothers listen:
"My lords," he says, "we need no lengthy discourse!
The King abides at Chalon town this minute,
And close to us is the whole Mâcon district;
Let us set forth and seize hold of the city!   2140
From Charles's hand with our own strength we'll strip it!"
But Garin says: "By my soul, I forbid it,
For that would be by our treason and trickery!
Let us instead speak with the King and win him!"
At this, behold two envoys of the King then,   2145
Baldwin and Hugh their names, come riding in there!
Up to the hall they climb the steps, where swiftly
They seek Girart and speak to him as bidden:
"Give ear, Girart, to Charlemagne's own wishes!
A good five years and more it is, we think it,   2150
Since Charles gave you this palace and this city;
Since then not one spur's worth in wealth you've given;
Now he sends you his word, which we deliver:
Come to him straight in homage and contrition!
If you do not, by St. Simon, know this much: 2155
He will come here and bring his army with him,
To burn your fields and turn your fief to cinders!
You'll not have left one button's worth of riches."
Girart hears this and all his whiskers bristle:
"Upon my soul, we'll go," says Garin quickly: 2160

"And we shall take one score of knights there with us,
The wisest we can find in all this kingdom,
   To judge the right and wrong."

60

Their council ends as I have told you each;
Then Hernaut says: "Will you come, Aymeri,   2165
To speak with Charles the King, abiding near
With all his knights? Among them you may see
Some of those men who heard the tale revealed
To you in boast that evening by the Queen."
"In God's name, lord," replies young Aymeri: 2170
"I shall find there thirteen, I guarantee!"
When this is said, those valiant knights all leave;
But Aymeri, whose mettle was not meek,
Speaks to an envoy in private ere he leaves:
"My friend," he says, "I bid you with all speed   2175
To summon all our men armed for the field,
And send them after us at my decree!
For I know well and doubt not in the least
That we'll leave Charles's court his enemies!"
The youth replies: "I'll do it, willingly."   2180
When this is said, those valiant knights all leave,
Their reins unchecked till Chalon town is reached;
Outside the walls a lodging-place they seek,
Then go to court all mindful of their need;
The King greets them with grace when they appear: 2185
"Fine, noble knights, welcome to all and each —
I am well pleased that you have come to me!"
"In truth, you ill deserve it," Sir Hernaut speaks:
"Accursed is he who holds your friendship dear!"
The King hears this and is heart-sick indeed;   2190
He looks the other way to Aymeri:
"Fine, well-bred youth, I bid you welcome here;
Not long ago I saw you, at St. Denis!"
The youth replies: "In the Lord's name, my liege,
Some thirty blows my welcome face received,   2195
Which I shall not forget for many a year;
The Queen herself showed me such love and peace

That I was nearly slain — it was quite clear
I had no friend among the Frenchmen here;
Soon as I could I turned my back to leave   2200
   And rode off to Vienne."

61

The Emperor hears all they have to tell;
Beside him sits the Queen in great distress;
He looks at her and his regard is dread;
He looks across at fierce-faced Girart then;   2205
Before his court he calls to him and says:
"My lord Girart, let nothing be unsaid:
Are all these knights of your household and realm?
Who is the old knight there, so white of head?"
"True Emperor, by Mary's son I pledge   2210
That is my father, whom may Lord Jesus bless,
And there are my three brothers, all powerful men;
Fine King, my lord, as you have heard from them,
Set me to right for the shameful contempt
Shown by the Queen in her proud foolishness   2215
Within the rooms of good Abbot Heles."
The King hears this, in no mood now to jest;
With ringing voice he calls his seneschal:
"Enquire for me and do not hide your quest,
If there is truth or mad deceitfulness   2220
In this complaint which I have heard alleged;
By all my faith in Mary's son, I pledge
I shall do more than any, if it's correct;
But if it's not, then let it be known hence
That from great good may spring great wickedness;   2225
For since the hour I gave Girart Vienne
And gave the rich Geneva to Renier,
They've paid me naught in service or in wealth;
But now I swear by Heaven's King Himself,
That I shall not set foot out of this realm   2230
Till one has paid for their deceitfulness!"
Says Aymeri: "May God bless me and let
The vengeance fall ere this day's sun has set!
Lord Emperor, I'll not leave this unsaid:

I pledge by God the well adored and blest,   2235
That there is none of mother born to breath,
No King or Prince of such pride and prowess,
Whom I would rate a rotten apple, when
He'd served me well only to shame me hence;
Though you gave me all of Romagna's wealth,   2240
I'll make no truce or peace, nor will relent
Until disgrace shall fall on this Queen's head;
  Ill-starred was her proud gesture!"

62

"My lord Girart," suggests the wise knight Naimes:
"Take wealth in coin by way of reparation!"   2245
Girart replies: "Your words and breath are wasted;
For by the Saint whom sinners seek and pray to,
Though you gave me Milan, I would not take it;
Nor Rome, Pavia, nor great Toulouse would make me
Grant my assent or any way placate me   2250
Till such revenge as I deem fit is taken
Upon this Queen, whose arrogant behavior
Brought me such shame and fills my heart with hatred!
And by that Saint whom sinners seek to save them,
I shall not stop while I have breath remaining,   2255
  Till she knows shame herself."

63

"My lord Girart," Naimes the duke persists:
"Allow the Queen atonement for her sin!
Let her lift up your saddle-bows so rich
Upon her head and walk one league therewith,   2260
Unshod and in a hair-shirt, if you so wish."
Garin replies: "You speak of pardon still;
But by the Saint they seek on Nero's hill,
We shall accept no peace or truce until
Her head and heart are parted for what she did."   2265
Says Do of Laon: "What the devil is this?
Who is this lord of hoary beard and lip,
Who speaks to us so wildly of his will?

I do defy him on behalf of the King!"
And he strides forth like one of wicked will   2270
And seizes hold of Garin by the chin;
One hundred hairs he plucks out of his skin,
    Before all of those barons.

64

Milon of Puglia's cheeks burn up with rage
To see his father's beard plucked in this way;   2275
He looks at Do with eyes of deepest hate,
While Renier of Geneva flings off his cape
And Duke Girart unsheathes his good, steel blade;
Young Aymeri is bearing a large mace
And he runs up to Do at a great pace   2280
And strikes the man without one moment's waste,
Who had plucked forth his grandsire's beard of gray;
He splits his head and down spurt all his brains;
The King cries out as loudly as he may:
"My household knights, take hold of him, I say!   2285
If you do not, you have betrayed your faith;
Try what he may, this knave shall not escape;
    He has disgraced my presence."

65

Some twenty five stand there before King Charles
Born to the clan of the brave knight Girart,   2290
And all are armed with sword or with a staff;
Unless the hall and palace fall apart,
I think they'll fight right through the French and pass;
Hernaut the count strikes Oton first and fast:
Beneath his chin his head and shoulders part;   2295
Then Miles of Puglia strikes Haguenan
Upon the skull with two blows of his staff;
And Renier of Geneva strikes Hoel hard;
And Girart swings his axe in a great arc,
Whose blade in length is one foot and a half;   2300
They leave the hall, whoever grieves or laughs;
And if the Queen had been where they went past,

Then their revenge, I'd say, would have been harsh;
But she is in her room, filled with alarm;
Those valiant knights pass by into the yard   2305
And to the spot where their good stallions are;
They mount their steeds without a backward glance;
On every side the Frenchmen seize their arms;
They would be mad to wait ere they depart —
    For they've committed outrage.   2310

66

In the good town the Frenchmen seize their weapons
As Girart's band ride off in rank well-serried;
Yer ere they've gone one half a league together,
Girart looks up between a plain and meadow
And sees his men arriving in great plenty,   2315
Led by the lad to whom they were commended!
They bear aloft St. Maurice's own ensign;
Girart sees them and cannot hide his pleasure;
He calls his brothers and looks at them and tells them:
"My lords, hear what I truly think this beckons: 2320
God shows His hand by sending them to help us!
I know in truth that these troops are our brethren,
    Who've ventured from Vienne."

67

When Girart meets with his own troops once more,
He starts to speak in a loud, ringing voice: 2325
"My worthy men, who set you on this course?"
"I did, my lord," says Aymeri the boy:
"Through an envoy I told this very morn."
Girart replies: "Nephew, I love you more!
If not for you, we'd all be killed or caught."   2330
The worthy band rides onward as before,
While fierce-faced Charles pursues them without pause,
With well-armed knights and men one hundred score;
Hermer of Paris rides out before them all
And starts to speak in a loud, ringing voice: 2335
"Where are you running to, Marquis Girart?

I challenge you, Renier of Geneva:
You are a thief and hostile to our Lord,
And to King Charles of St. Denis show false!"
Renier hears this and his blood almost boils;   2340
He shouts at him: "You lie, son of a whore!
And I am ready to prove to you and all
That I have never betrayed the Emperor!"
When this is said, they wait for nothing more;
With their great spurs they goad their stallions forth;   2345
On his dark shield the shaft of Renier bores
Above the boss and breaks his buckler's boards;
His coat's not worth a lily-leaf once torn:
Into his ribs the heavy lance-head gores
And on the slope he's flung dead from his horse;   2350
Good Renier grips his fine horse as he falls
And then rides back as a well-bred knight ought:
"In God's name, uncle Renier," Aymeri calls:
"I love you more than ever I did before!
If you give me this worthy horse you've brought,   2355
Then I'll be armed and mounted fit for war
As a new knight to fight for our good cause;
     In my honest opinion."

68

To dub as knight the noble Aymeri
They all dismount within a glade well-leafed;   2360
Girart the duke and all his brothers three
Place on his back the mail of triple-weave
And on his head the burnished helm of green;
Girart girds on his sword of polished steel
And with his palm a solid blow he beats: 2365
"Be valiant, Aymeri, and think of me!"
The lad replies: "I thank you much, my liege;
I shall, if I may live and if God please."
Then they lead out to him an Arab steed
And he, waiting no more, mounts up the beast;   2370
About his neck they hang a strong, curved shield,
And in his hand he grips a burnished spear;
He runs his horse across the flowery field

And each one says: "How fine a knight is he!"
The valiant knights give blessing all and each,   2375
    With joy and great rejoicing.

69

The well-bred Aymeri is dubbed a knight;
He bears the arms and armor for the first time;
The band rides on, not wasting any time,
For Charles the King is now not far behind   2380
And in his ranks a good two thousand ride;
Young Aymeri's a brave and well-bred child:
He turns his good Norwegian steed to strike
One Jocerain, who comes from Albi's shire;
He splits his shield and hauberk's folds aside   2385
And rams his ribs with valiant Vienne iron;
He spears him well then flings him dead and cries:
"You'll come no closer now to me and mine!"
He turns his reins, not wasting any time,
But seizes first the good horse as his prize,   2390
    And gives it to his uncle.

70

The count rides on with no further delay —
For Charles the King, whose beard is white with age,
Pursues him hard with all the haste he may,
And in his ranks ride knights of France the famed;   2395
See Renier face them now across a vale!
His worthy horse has galloped hard all day:
He has spurred it to run time and again;
Renier looks up at those coming their way
And turns the head of his good horse to face   2400
One Eliot with all his strength and hate;
Before the rest he moves to strike straightway:
He splits his shield without one moment's waste
And his white coat is soon cleft of its chains;
Right through his ribs he threads his battle-gage;   2405
From his gold seat he flings him to his grave
In front of Charles, whose beard is gray with age;

Then he takes his good steed by its gold reins
And comes to Lord Girart and wisely says:
"We'll not outfight them here — let us escape!"   2410
When this is said, they spur their steeds and race
    Headlong for Vienne city.

71

Charles and his knights pursue them hard and well;
Clutched in his hand Charles holds a rod erect
As on he rides and calls aloud and says: 2415
"Where do you run, Girart, you lowly wretch?
You shall not see this selfsame season end,
Ere I'll besiege your castle at Vienne!
If I take you, no ransom will be set —
I shall have you with chains around your neck!"   2420
Says Aymeri: "This is a foolish threat!
I'll not conceal from you Girart's intent:
He'll strike your hide with his sharp lance's head
And thrust the gonfalon right through your flesh,
Whoever grieves at this or makes lament!"   2425
The knights of both attack when this is said,
And Girart's ranks straightway lose fifty men;
Our Emperor turns back to Vaudon then,
Whose waters flow with mighty tow and depth;
And Girart comes to his fort in Vienne;   2430
The Queen herself, of visage fair and fresh,
Returns to France, and when back in that realm,
Calls forth at once a mighty force of men;
From all around they come when summoned hence,
Soldiers and squires, fifteen thousand of them;   2435
The Queen of France leads them at once to help
    King Charlemagne her husband.

72

Straight to Vienne, as evening draws near,
Comes Duke Girart with all his men of liege;
Upon the stone they step down from their steeds,   2440
Whence to the hall of marbled walls they reach;

Girart hails all his mighty kin and speaks:
"My lords," he says, "to my own thoughts give ear:
King Charles of France has turned his hate on me;
This day so many men of mine he's seized   2445
Whom I'll not see again ere long, I fear!"
Then Renier cries: "I swear by Christ's own creed,
King Charles shall not, I pledge you truthfully,
Set foot in France or have one moment's peace,
Till he had paid most dearly for his deeds!   2450
For by the Saint they seek in Nero's field,
When we have slain and lain him in his bier,
We'll crown as King of France young Aymeri!"
"Brother," says Miles, "that is an ill-made speech!
Majestic God forbids us all and each   2455
To speak in pride or foolish vanity;
Charles is a valiant man, all know this here;
There is no finer King on earth than he;
If he should die, I swear by Christ's own creed,
The whole of France would rise up in its grief;   2460
To rob the King of all of Burgundy
Would be revenge enough, it seems to me;
To go to France would be a foolish scheme —
    It's full of fearsome fighters."

73

At dawn's first light, with arms and armor on,   2465
Girart's great force of knights and men set off
From Vienne town, the sturdy and well-stocked;
They ride in ranks some twenty thousand strong;
Between the woods and the surrounding rocks
They seize the herds belonging to Mâcon,   2470
Then take the town itself by force and shock;
What wealth they find behind the city's locks —
Almerian silks and sundry precious cloths,
And gold and silver and steeds of Syrian stock!
Girart's great lords lead all this booty off   2475
Straight to Vienne, the sturdy and well-stocked;
An envoy leaves Mâcon and does not stop
Till he finds Charles of whiskers white and long,
    And tells him these new tidings.

74

The envoy leaves and urgently he rides   2480
Upon a steed which sweats from head to hind;
At a great pace he races down the heights
And does not halt till Charles's lodge is nigh;
He asks for Charles and they show him inside;
As soon as he beholds the King he cries: 2485
"King Charlemagne, heed well this news of mine!
Your town Mâcon is taken from you, Sire;
Of all its wealth the little that survives
Would not amount to two deniers entire."
The King hears this and rages almost wild: 2490
"Who has done this?" says Charlemagne the wise:
"In God's name, lord, their names I will not hide!
Girart the duke and Duke Renier the wise
And Miles of Puglia and all their line;
From Tarentaise up to Genèvre's heights   2495
There is no evil Lombard or Puglian knight
Whom they have not secured to their own might,
     To help them and support them."

75

"I'll hide nothing from you," proceeds the envoy:
"Fine King, my lord, pay heed to what I tell you;   2500
Both Duke Girart and his brother Duke Milon
Have openly and in great haste assembled
All of their men from every town and dwelling;
And what is more, their good brother Sir Hernaut
Has brought a host of Toulouse men to help them;   2505
They have all sworn in highest rage and temper
To take from you no reparation ever,
But to lay waste all of your French possessions,
So that no wealth of one spur's worth is left you —
Unless you give the Queen of fair complexion   2510
Into their hands, so they may take their vengeance."
When Charles hears this, no heart was ever so heavy;
He calls to him two lords, Droon and Hervi,
And says: "My lords, how foul a wrong besets me!
Girart the duke, whom in my hall I welcomed   2515

And made a knight, has proved a thankless felon!
I urge you both to go to France as envoys
And bring back here Baldwin and Hugh, together
With young Roland of bright and fair complexion:
In all of France let there remain no Frenchman,   2520
No knight, no foot-soldier, none with a weapon,
Who does not come to Vienne town directly;
Those without weapons we shall provide in plenty."
The pair reply: "With the Almighty's blessing,
True Emperor, your will shall be our pleasure."   2525
And they ride back, as fast as spurs will fetch them,
To seek from France the aid that Charles has sent for;
In the meantime, with no delay, the Emperor
Bids brought to him St. Simon's reliquary;
And Charles and all his knights swear on the relics   2530
That he'll lay siege to Vienne's stout defenses;
His siege may last for fourteen years ere ever
    He'll take that hall by force!

76

The messengers have gone to France the sweet;
They muster up a mighty host indeed;   2535
Those in Vienne say their farewells and leave:
Milon of Puglia departs for his demesne,
And to his noble town of Biaulande speeds
Hernaut once more, of strength and temper fierce;
And Renier goes back to his town Geneve;   2540
Girart remains inside his hall at ease,
For the good duke cannot at all believe
That Charles will come and make war on him here:
And yet, within the course of one short year,
One hundred men will die during the siege;   2545
Those messengers whose names I have revealed,
Who went to France at Charlemagne's decree,
Have stayed at length within that land to lead
So great a force of men back to the field
That never yet had France sent forth its peer;   2550
Of five score thousand men the record speaks,
Some dukes, some counts, some knights of high degree;

They tarry not, they set out on their steeds
And ride so far together at a good speed
Till on a Tuesday they enter Burgundy; 2555
Beside a hill they camp for one night's sleep,
And the next day, when dawn breaks bright and clear,
They take the road to Mâcon in good cheer,
     And Charles rides forth to meet them.

77

Through Burgundy in haste the Emperor rides; 2560
Towards the west he turns and sets his eyes
Upon sweet France, the worthy and the prized;
He sees the ranks upon the steep hillside
And blesses them with God Almighty's sign:
"Ah God!" he says, "Our fine and royal Sire, 2565
How happy should he be to be alive,
Who can command a force of men so fine!
Now by the Saint whom sinners seek to find,
Since I have pledged my word and sworn to Christ,
I shall not enter brave France again till I 2570
     Have captured Vienne city!"

78

That night King Charlemagne sleeps in the field
Until next day when dawn breaks bright and clear;
On every side the army wakes from sleep
And packs its arms upon those sumpter-beasts; 2575
Straight for Mâcon they ride with their best speed,
For they themselves believe quite certainly
That in the town they'll still find Aymeri;
But he is wise and when he first perceived
The mighty ranks which Charles had had convened, 2580
And all the knights whom Charles had made to meet,
The brave lad left for Vienne town in brief,
Which, it was clear, was his safest retreat;
When he learns this, Charles rides hot on his heels
With his great ranks and barons all and each; 2585
He orders carts to carry wines and wheat

And on all sides he lays Vienne to siege;
They set up tents, pavilions and marquees:
And yet this siege may last for five long years
Before they'll take this mighty castle's keep;   2590
For this whole town is richly stocked indeed,
  And those inside are valiant.

79

Great is the siege laid all around Vienne:
No man alive has seen a greater set;
The King of St. Denis speaks forth his pledge   2595
Not to depart till he takes all of them;
Girart the duke sees all his walls beset,
And wonder not if he is filled with dread:
"Lord God, fine King of Paradise," he says:
"I shall be slain, if I can gain no help;   2600
In Puglia bides Count Milon the well-bred,
And fierce Hernaut is in Biaulande again,
And brave Renier is back in Geneva."
And so he calls upon three messengers;
Girart the marquis says: "Attend me well!   2605
Tomorrow morn, when dawn's first light is shed,
You three must leave without delay or let
To seek help from my brothers and other friends;
Tell them that Charles has laid siege to Vienne;
For love of Him Whom Longinus confessed,   2610
Bid them to come and help me in this realm."
"My lord," they say, "we shall do all you've said."
"In God's name, uncle," young Aymeri says then:
"I shall not eat, my solemn word I pledge,
Till I have slain some knight among the French   2615
And by myself have taken prisoners!"
Girart replies: "Nephew, God be your help!
Without you here my heart would be distressed."
He takes his arms, the youth brave and well-bred;
He dons his coat and laces his bright helm;   2620
A strong, curved shield they drape around his neck
And in his hand a shining spear they set;
He summons forth more knights five score and ten

And through the gate they go with fierce intent;
In Charles's host they hear them coming thence   2625
And arms are seized by two hundred of them;
There are no cries from either side of men,
But each spurs forth to meet with fierce intent,
And on their shields the shock of each is felt;
The big shafts hit and bits fly in the air;   2630
The fight begins and bitterly it spreads;
The lances break and shields are shorn and bent
And knights are felled from their rich destriers;
Amid the crush young Aymeri's hard pressed;
With ringing voice he cries aloud and yells: 2635
"God shame the man who does not strike his best!"
Marquis Girart is in his tower, when
He hears his nephew's cry among the press
And the great blows as men fight to the death;
So he arms up his bravest knights and men,   2640
Some twenty-seven of his courageous best,
And through the gate they go with fierce intent;
But Charles's host do not at all see them,
As Girart's force rides swiftly to their tents
And swing their blades of steel and burnished edge;   2645
With bitter blows the fighting starts again:
See many a solid shield of boards all bent
And many a coat of mail all ripped and rent
And many a knight knocked from his mount to death!
They hack to ground the Frenchmen's biggest tent,   2650
Where Charles of St. Denis lies on his bed;
But when the King hears swords strive with their strength
And strike upon those green and burnished helms,
He leaves his bed and goes to Bernart's tent,
    Calling for arms and armor.   2655

80

To Bernart's tent the Emperor escapes
And leaves his own so that he may keep safe;
And then the Queen, of bright and shining face,
Flees after him from her own tent in haste;
But Aymeri, he grasps her by the waist,   2660

And Girart's joy, on seeing this, is great!
From his left hip he draws his worthy blade
To strike her down in all his rage and hate;
But Aymeri, with ringing voice exclaims:
"Uncle Girart, don't kill her, for God's sake!   2665
To Vienne fort let her be led away
Where we may wreak such vengeance as we crave!"
Girart replies, "You're wise in what you say."
See Roland then, King Charles's nephew brave,
And Baldwin too, who is well-bred the same;   2670
They are both nephews of Laon's King Charlemagne;
Baldwin speaks first to Charlemagne and says:
"True Emperor, we tarry here too late!
The Queen, I think, is lost to us this day:
To Vienne fort Girart's hauled her away;   2675
Help her, my lord, for God's sake and His name!"
"Most willingly I will," says Charlemagne,
And leaps astride his Gascon destrier,
Not fully armed, he leaves in such a haste;
Around his neck a lion-shield is draped,   2680
While in his fist a solid spear he shakes;
He leaves the tent and spurs as fast he may
Upon his steed to give Duke Girart chase,
Whose plan it is to place the Queen in chains;
The King sees Aymeri clutching her waist   2685
And smites his lion-painted shield straightway;
He breaks its boards beneath the blazon's paint;
The hauberk's strong, he cannot pierce the mail,
But strikes him well and flings him on the plain;
He takes the Queen, of bright and shining face,   2690
And bids her mount a Gascon destrier;
He leads her back to Bernart's tent again,
     And from a death most certain.

81

Back to Vienne rides Girart from the sortie,
With Aymeri, the young lad fine and lordly,   2695
And all of those who'd left with them that morning;
They have sown fear among King Charles's forces

For they have slain or put in chains some forty!
Girart dismounts at last from his good war-horse
And, sick at heart, he strides into his hallway: 2700
"By Your blest power, Lord Jesus, I exhort you —
If I receive no help, my life is forfeit!
Miles is in Puglia, to my misfortune,
And white-headed Hernaut is back in Biaulande,
And in Geneva is fearsome Renier also; 2705
Too late shall be the aid they could afford me!"
But Duke Girart is sick at heart for naught, lords!
For the next morn, when daylight is just dawning,
Milon of Puglia has much help for him —
One thousand men with shields to show he's brought him, 2710
And from another side Hernaut rides forward
With one thousand brave men equipped for warfare;
Renier's recalled all his Genevan warlords
And come to help as a fine warrior ought to,
With two thousand good men on long-maned horses; 2715
And one of his own sons this time has joined him:
Young Oliver, Roland's beloved henceforward;
Till reaching there the brothers have not halted,
And now they all dismount before the fortress;
To see them there fills Girart with rejoicing 2720
And he goes from his gate and rides towards them;
He kisses each as each appears before him;
He looks at Oliver, there to support him,
And lovely Aude, whose presence makes him joyful,
And round their necks he hugs both of them warmly; 2725
The squires run off to ready lodgings for them
And stable well their good long-maned war-horses;
Girart the duke climbs up to his high hallway
With all his brothers whom he has cherished always;
The valiant knights climb to the upper storeys 2730
And there survey the host encamped before them;
See Roland now, who'd ridden out beforehand
Below Vienne, bearing his hunting-falcon
Down to the Rhône, and seen drakes on the water;
The fearsome youth had launched his hawk towards them, 2735
Which caught two ducks and felled two drakes it caught there;
But then the bird had vanished in an orchard;

When Oliver sees this, he can't ignore it;
He speaks aloud and is well heard by all there:
"By God, uncle, here's a piece of good fortune: 2740
A noble youth has gone from the French forces
Down to the Rhône beneath Vienne on horseback;
His hunting-hawk has downed two drakes in sport there,
Then flown away into that leafy orchard:
If I can't catch that bird, then I'm a poor one!   2745
And I'll not give it back, when I have caught it,
    For love of these French knights!"

82

Girart replies: "Fine nephew, let this be!
If I lost you, my happiness would cease!"
Says Oliver: "You waste your words, my liege!   2750
I'll go, though I should lose one of my feet!"
Upon his horse he mounts with utmost speed
And through the gate in a great haste he leaves;
He does not stop till he comes to those trees
And finds the bird perched on a branch well-leafed;   2755
He sets the hawk upon his left-hand's sleeve;
Roland sees this and fills with rage indeed;
With ringing voice he cries aloud and clear:
"Are you an envoy, boy? Don't lie to me!
Give me back now the falcon I hold dear!   2760
I'll see you paid some fifteen pounds in fee."
Says Oliver: "Yours is a wasted plea!
One hundred pounds in gold won't set it free!
You seem a money-lender, judged by your speech,
Who think that coin can pay for what you lease!   2765
Go buy a bird! This one belongs to me!"
Roland hears this and all his senses reel;
He rides his horse straight through the river's stream
And on the other bank comes to those trees;
By both the reins he grasps Oliver's steed   2770
And speaks to Oliver in courtly speech:
"What is your name? Don't hide it or conceal!"
"My lord, my name is Oliver," says he:
"I am Count Renier's son, born in Geneve;

And brave Hernaut is an uncle to me,   2775
As is Girart, Count of Vienne, the fierce,
Whom Charles intends to chase out of his fief,
   Most evilly and wrongly."

83

When Oliver hears Roland's fearsome talk,
He says to him in a fine, courtly voice: 2780
"I have told you my name and kin, young lord;
Now, who are you? Do not hide it at all."
"My friend," he says to him, "Roland I'm called,
Nephew of Charles, our mighty Emperor;
Now by the Saint of those pilgrims besought,   2785
If God permits and His will still accords
That I may pass again onto this shore,
Girart shall die with the gray-haired Hernaut;
I'll hang them up to the four winds with joy!
Give back my bird — take it not one step more!   2790
I do not wish that some young boy should vaunt
That he robbed me of the least bezant coin!"
Says Oliver: "To me such words mean naught;
Pay heed to me and be my squire henceforth;
If I am pleased with you in my employ,   2795
Within a year, I'd say, you can be sure
That I shall make a town or region yours
Or give to you a rich city or fort,
   As you seem worthy of it."

84

When Roland hears Oliver speak this way,   2800
He lifts his fist to strike him straightaway;
But suddenly a thought enters his brain
Which makes him stop and speak to him again:
"Vassal, once more I ask of you," he says:
"To give me back my falcon with good grace,   2805
And with this bargain, which you shall hear me make:
If you require a favor of me one day,
I shall give you whatever your heart craves."

Says Oliver: "This bargain is well made;
With these terms set, this bird is yours to take!"   2810
He frees the straps with which it is restrained
And Roland takes the bird without delay;
Young Oliver calls out to him and says:
"By all the faith you owe to Charlemagne,
Your mighty uncle, for whom your love is great,   2815
If I had wanted to take your bird away,
Don't hide from me how you would have behaved!"
"I will tell you the truth," Roland exclaims:
"By the Saint sought in Nero's field, I say
I would have hurled my whole fist in your face   2820
With so much strength, whomever this dismays,
That both your eyes would have flown through the air,
    With all your kinsmen watching."

85

Oliver glows like coals when he hears this;
With angry voice he answers thus to him: 2825
"Vassal, would I have stood still while you did?
You're no taller than I, nor stronger built;
By the blest Saint they seek on Nero's hill,
If ever we two fought, I tell you this:
You would not boast in France that you had stripped   2830
Sir Oliver of one button or bit!
I would not need to wield a sword or stick;
I'd punch your nose so hard with my whole fist
That the bright blood would flow down fast and thick,
    With all the siege-host watching!"   2835

86

"Wretch!" Roland says, "God curse you for your lies!
By the great Lord Whom we should praise on High,
If I were back in camp, equipped to fight,
Then Count Girart and all his breed would die!
I'll hang them all before four months are by,   2840
And your hair shall be shaved and shorn awry,
And you shall be the butt of jest and jibes!

And yet, I shall return your grace in kind,
For giving back this hunting-hawk of mine:
You shall not die — I'll give you back your life!"   2845
When Oliver hears this, this much he plights:
"By the Saint sought in Nero's field, if I
Live long enough to be received a knight,
And if I meet with you in battle's strife,
I'll strike so hard with my nielloed pike   2850
That if you are not felled, I'll wonder why!"
Roland hears this and laughs in his face twice;
He spurs his steed and through the stream he strikes
And presses through and out the other side;
Past all the tents and lodges there he rides;   2855
Before the King down in the field he lights;
Around him come his noblest men and knights:
The King himself speaks out when he arrives;
"Give ear to me," he says, "my nephew fine;
Who is that youth, tell me and do not hide,   2860
To whom you spoke beyond this water wide?"
"By God, you'll hear the truth," Roland replies:
"He is Count Renier's son, Geneva's sire,
And a nephew of wild Girart likewise."
The King hears this and almost leaves his mind: 2865
"You fool! Why did you not kill him?" he cries:
"By the good God, Who is called Jesus Christ,
I have no wish that he should live and thrive,
And that his deeds should glorify his line!"
"In God's name, Sire," the brave Roland replies: 2870
"I had no armor on or steel to strike
A blow at him or take his blow alike."
Says Charlemagne: "Nephew, your words are wise;
 Ride out no more unready!"

87

Straight to Vienne without delay returns   2875
Young Oliver, that youth of so much worth;
Girart sees him and calls him with these words:
"My nephew fine, has your courage been curbed?
Your luck was in, thank God and His good works,

Or you'd have been hauled off a prisoner!   2880
I saw you by that bridge where you rode first,
And on your fist you bore a falcon-bird;
From the French host I saw a youngster surge
Straight through the flood, like a brave knight he spurred
And took the hawk, whatever you preferred;   2885
How good's a hound with the heart of a cur?
No man henceforth should hold your valor dear!"
When Oliver hears this, his visage burns
And he says to Girart, angry and hurt:
"In Lord God's name, you speak of valor, sir,   2890
Like a rich man of such breeding and birth
Who kissed the claw of Charles's Queen, when urged!
She boasted this and many a baron heard
At St. Denis in Abbot Heles's church;
By my faith in St. Simon, this galls me worse,   2895
    For its great shame destroys me."

88

When Girart sees his nephew so distressed,
He takes him to his father, Count Renier,
Who greets the pair and kisses both of them:
"In God's name, lord," young Oliver requests: 2900
"I need a horse and arms and armor next;
For I am lithe and have good health and strength,
And in a joust I wish to prove myself
And be a knight and put myself to test."
"Nephew, I grant you this," Duke Girart says: 2905
"You shall have all with my willing consent."
So all's prepared without delay or let:
With every haste young Oliver is dressed
In shirt and hose and shoes from Montpellier;
Upon his back a rich, white fur they set   2910
Above a tunic tailored to fit him well;
They lead him then to church, where Mass is said,
As is the custom when a new knight is blessed:
Ere he may wield his arms in cause or quest,
He must hear Mass and pray for Lord God's help   2915
To grant him honor and to bring him success

And let him rule with justice and good sense;
When Mass is said, back to the hall he's led
And clad once more in knighthood's gear and dress;
Upon his back a white hauberk they set,   2920
And on his head a green and golden helm;
Girart girds to his side a blade sharp-edged,
Then beats a solid blow upon his neck:
"Remember me and be brave, Oliver!"
"I thank you much, my lord," the brave lad says: 2925
"I shall, if I may live and have God's help!"
Then they bring him a rapid destrier
And he steps in its stirrup on the left,
While worthy squires upon the right attend;
When this is done, a quartered shield is fetched   2930
And in his fist a cutting spear is set,
Which bears a flag fixed to its upper end;
If you could see him wielding his shield then,
Shortening the straps to brace it to his breast,
Trying his steed throughout the courtway's length   2935
And galloping off to ride among the French!
Each say to each: "How fine a knight goes there!
God keep him safe, the guardian of all men!"
Renier prays this above all of the rest;
Sir Oliver does not delay, instead   2940
He comes to Duke Girart with this request:
"My lord, I will not hide what I'd attempt:
Outside these walls I'd seek my pleasure hence;
God may grant me success in some event
Which in your eyes may raise my estimate!"   2945
Renier, his father, says: "You'll not go yet!
If I lost you by any chance ill-met,
No man alive would make me smile again!"
"Yes, he shall go!" the warrior Girart says:
"No man should hold him back from his prowess!   2950
God keep him safe, the guardian of all men!"
Young Oliver turns round, when this is said,
And through the gate he rides out of Vienne;
Beside the walls he spurs his horse ahead
And does not ride an arrow's distance, when   2955
He sees a knight leave from the siege-host's tents,

Who is the praised and much-prized Guinement;
Beneath Vienne he rides on pleasure bent,
Armed and equipped on a swift destrier
To prove his worth, his bravery and strength;   2960
When Oliver sees him there by himself,
He spurs his horse towards him, fierce and dread;
He does not deign to challenge him, instead
He strikes him hard upon his buckler's edge;
Beneath the boss he splits the shield to shreds   2965
And the hauberk beneath he rips and rends
And through his ribs the spear of steel he sends;
He smites him well and flings him to his death;
Into the sand he rams his helmet's edge,
Then by the reins he takes his destrier   2970
And turns around like one brave and well bred;
His father, Duke Renier, fills with content,
As does Girart, the brave lord of Vienne;
But on the other side what anger spreads
Among the host in fierce-faced Charles's tents —   2975
For Guinement's a knight bred of the best,
Who has been robbed of horse and life as well!
But now, my lords, I'll leave Sir Oliver,
And in due course I'll tell of him again;
I'll tell you now what brave Roland does next: 2980
He calls for arms and armor for himself,
Which willingly they find for him and fetch;
Upon his back a white hauberk they set
And gird his sword Durendal on his left;
They lead him out a rapid destrier   2985
Whose stirrups he steps into upon the left;
A quartered shield they hang around his neck
And then he grips a sturdy lance steel-edged;
A worthy knight he looks in all respects;
The French look on, all knights of high prowess,   2990
And each one says: "We should prize this one well:
There's none on earth who looks so fierce or dread;
God keep him safe, the guardian of all men;
    For he seems very noble."

89

Roland is armed in a most splendid fashion;   2995
He spurs his steed down through the Frenchmen's campsite;
Young Aymeri bides in Vienne's great palace,
His heart on fire to joust his foe in battle;
He calls for arms and armor from his clansmen
And they are brought straightway for him to have them;   3000
His coat of mail he dons and helmet flashing
And girds his blade with its bright, golden handle;
They bring to him a strong and lively stallion,
And stopping not he steps into its saddle;
About his neck a heavy shield is hanging,   3005
And in his hand a cutting spear is brandished;
Out of the gate he goes now at a gallop;
Upon his way he meets Roland the valiant;
They neither speak nor send each other challenge,
But strike great blows upon each buckler's panels;   3010
Beneath the boss the boards of each are shattered;
Their coats are strong, the chain-mail is undamaged;
Roland is fierce and a knight of great valor;
On Aymeri he lands a blow so massive
That it brings down the youth from his fierce stallion;   3015
Then Roland grasps its silver reins, to catch it,
And leads it off in a most courtly manner,
    With all of Vienne watching.

90

When Aymeri is felled upon all fours,
He leaps straight up and grasps his buckler broad;   3020
Then he draws forth his burnished, sharp-edged sword
And cries aloud: "Sir knight, why now withdraw?
If you depart, all of your fame will fall!"
Roland replies: "Be gone yourself, young lord!
Since I have felled you once, I'll do no more;   3025
But I shall take this lively, long-maned horse!"
When Aymeri hears this, his heart is galled;
Back to Vienne he comes, and he must walk;
When Oliver sees this, he fills with joy;
He finds Girart and brings him this report,   3030

Well heard by all, in a clear, ringing voice:
"Uncle, I've seen a wonder, by God the Lord!
Aymeri's joust dismays me not at all —
The same vassal has won who took my hawk!
I've never seen, nor has there been before   3035
    A knight of France his equal."

Part Three:
The Siege of Vienne

91

Listen, my lords, may Lord God bless you all,
The glorious One of blessèd Mary born!
No foolishness or lies do I record
But valiant deeds and true from times of yore, 3040
And battles fierce and heavy, hard-fought wars;
In all his life Charles never suffered more,
Except in Spain among the heathen Moors,
Where Roland was betrayed through spite and scorn,
With Oliver, the valiant-visaged lord, 3045
And twenty thousand Frenchmen were made to fall;
Now Charlemagne does not delay or halt;
Before Vienne, its ancient town and fort,
He sets up camp with all his sieging force;
They ravage land around and they assault 3050
Town after town with fire and with their swords;
They waste the vines and gather any spoils,
Oxen and cattle or any wealth or coin;
The people flee, they dare not stay indoors,
They leave their homes and the fields of their toil; 3055
The land around is left bereft and poor —
All of its wealth Charles takes for his own cause;
Yet he gains naught inside of Vienne's walls:
For seven years he stays there with his force
And does not move, for any wind or storm, 3060
    From sieging Vienne city.

92

Easter it is and summer is beginning:
The woods sprout leaves, the fields are green, and in them
The birds sweetly and merrily are singing;
King Charles resides in his royal pavilion   3065
Beneath Vienne, that admirable city;
Roland the duke from hunting now comes hither,
Out of a glade where he has stayed, and with him
Are many knights of valiant strength and visage;
Two stags and one wild-boar they've taken in there;   3070
Now Roland rides straight to the main pavilion;
He says straightway, when he beholds the King there:
"My lord and liege, I urge you please to listen!
Full seven years have run their course and finished
Since you laid siege to this most worthy city;   3075
Like ordered monks the men inside are living,
While we outside like stranded stags are milling!
Sire, if you please, let me with your permission
Set up outside the city walls a quintain;
The new-dubbed knights will strike the target swiftly,   3080
And agile youths from the French host will hit it,
And we shall see and be able to witness
Which of them all shall prove with arms most skillful
When battle comes and jousts are for the winning!"
Says Charles: "By God, fine nephew, I forbid it!   3085
I know too well the mighty pride of Girart!
With his best knights he would ride from the city —
Though he risked life and limb, he'd not resist it,
And he'd demand the first joust at the quintain!
A worthy man's oft thwarted by a villain!"   3090
Roland replies: "Let all that be, I bid you!
By all the faith that I owe you and give you,
I shall lead forth one thousand armed knights with me;
If Girart comes or brave Oliver visits,
They'll not return to Vienne town so quickly!   3095
With our steel blades we shall oppose them swiftly!"
Says Ganelon: "My lord, he truly will do!
A braver knight than Roland you'll not witness!"
Naimes supports the plea with so much vigor
That Charlemagne at last gives his permission: 3100

Roland can do whatever now he wishes
  To set his quintain up.

93

Naimes supports the plea with so much weight,
As do Count Ganelon and brave Ogier,
That Charlemagne at last says that he may;   3105
Roland the duke, at this, makes no delay:
Down in a field he sets up three stout stakes
And covers them with three strong suits of mail;
Then see those lithe-limbed youths prepare in haste!
See saddles set on many a destrier   3110
And pikes and spears seized in the hand and raised!
Inside Vienne bides Oliver the brave,
With lovely Aude, worthy of so much praise;
The well-bred knight looks down upon the plain
And sees there on the field a quintain raised;   3115
Pure gold galore could no more cheer his face,
And the good knight begins to plan straightway
How he make strike the quintain first that day!
He calls to him his squire Garin and says:
"Go saddle up my swift-paced destrier   3120
And bring to me my gear of dearest make,
For I would seek some sport outside the gate!"
Aude hears all this and holds him in embrace:
"Brother," she says, "where do you plan to play?"
"I'll join the French in joust, my fairest maid!"   3125
She says: "Do not do that, for good God's sake!
King Charles will have your head in his great hate,
Or Roland will, his nephew fierce and brave;
All the world's gold would be of no avail:
They would both hang you, if they should catch you there!"   3130
"Fair one," he says, "pray do not be dismayed,
For by the Lord, in Whose hands all are placed,
If Sir Girart finds out, and you're to blame,
Then you shall lose my love for you always!"
"My lord," she says, "speak no more of it, pray!   3135
I shall not breathe a word of it or phrase,
  For you are my dear brother."

94

He arms himself like a knight bravely bred:
Most splendidly he starts to dress himself
In silver spurs and iron upon his legs,   3140
A coat of mail and a bright, shining helm;
His cutting sword he girds upon his left;
A lively steed they lead out to him then,
Clad all in iron from its hind to its head;
The bridle's worth fourteen bright marks itself;   3145
The count mounts up without the pommel's help;
A heavy shield he drapes about his neck
And takes a pike with a stout, cutting edge;
Out of the postern-gate in haste he heads;
Swift as he can he mingles with the French   3150
To strike the quintain in the thick of the press,
Before he's known by Charles or by his men;
The maiden Aude, of worthy heart, is left
Weeping alone at a high window-ledge;
Her brother's fate she tenderly laments: 3155
"Oliver, brother, brave count of high prowess,
May God the Lord, of trust and truthfulness,
Safeguard you now from torment and from death;
For Charlemagne, the powerful Emperor,
Hates you indeed, as do all of his men."   3160
To Duke Girart an envoy quickly says
That Oliver, the count of high prowess,
Has left the town on his swift destrier,
Without a guard of soldiers or of friends;
Girart hears this and anger fills his breast;   3165
With fearsome rage he swears this solemn pledge:
"No knight or soldier shall stay inside Vienne,
Who can bear arms or any weapons hence!
Each, fully armed, shall leave with me to help;
Now I shall see those who will help me best!   3170
He who would hold his fief from me and wealth,
Let him in haste equip and arm himself,
And let us ride straightway to the French tents!
For I would show my temper and my strength
To Charles the King of all sweet France's realm."   3175
   "Your will be done!" reply all Girart's men:

"Who fails you here, fails his own honor's test!"
And so they arm, when these words have been said;
They don their hauberks and lace their shining helms,
And gird those swords of sharp and cutting edge,   3180
And heavy shields they drape about their necks;
Stout, cutting pikes they seize in hand, and then
They pass the gate in haste out of Vienne;
Girart the duke rides fiercely at their head
Upon a steed which gallops out unchecked;   3185
With gonfalons their lance-heads are bedecked,
And in the wind they billow down and spread;
Girart the duke leads all his knights and men
Into a lovely glade beneath Vienne;
There they keep watch, some three thousand of them,   3190
And the glade glows with the gold rays they shed;
Ere the ninth hour is heard, or vesper's bell,
A mighty loss by one side will be felt —
To Vienne's force or to the host of French,
    In joust below the city.   3195

95

Our Emperor, the King of St. Denis,
Calls to his side two knights of high degree:
One is Entelme, the other is Gaudris:
"My lords," he says, "to my advice give heed!
Go guard for me our quintain in the field   3200
So that Girart may not insult us here!"
They say: "We shall do as you wish, my liege."
But they'll not stop Count Oliver at least,
As by the straps he grasps hold of his shield
And sets it on his breast, so high and near   3205
That no French knight can pick him from their peers!
The valiant youth spurs forth his lively steed
Towards the quintain and strikes it lustily!
He splits the shields and slits the coats beneath
And breaks in half the holding-posts all three!   3210
Down in the field he fells all in a heap
As he rides through with an unbroken spear;
He has displayed his jousting-strength indeed!

Charles signs himself when he beholds this feat,
And calls on God, Who never fails in need: 3215
"Almighty Father, for grace! I've never seen
So stout a blow as I've just witnessed here!
Frenchmen, ride forth and find who it may be!
If he is noble, or soldiers for a fee,
Of all my wealth he may partake and keep!"   3220
The French reply: "As you desire, my liege!"
When this is said, some ten break ranks and leave,
Rich dukes and marquises are all of these;
When Oliver sees them, his enemies,
It is no wonder, lords , that he should fear;   3225
He turns the reins of his good, noble steed,
And shows his lance with its gonfalon reared;
The first to follow him he strikes with zeal,
Piercing his shield and triple coat beneath;
Right through his ribs he rams his cutting spear   3230
And flings him dead — what more could he achieve?
He cries: "Vienne! God's aid and St. Maurice!
I'm Oliver, no friend of yours, dead peer!
Girart, Hernaut — I am nephew of these;
My father is the noble Duke Renier,   3235
My sister, Aude, of visage fair and sweet;
Where are you, Roland, brave knight of daring deeds?
I'll vie with you on any battlefield!
Brave Aymeri would have you know, through me,
That he will not forgive or give you peace,   3240
For his steed's sake which yesterday you thieved!
He'll have revenge, as long as he still breathes!"
Roland looks down and Ganelon laughs deep:
"Ah God, true King of Paradise," Charles speaks:
"Full seven years have come and run their lease   3245
Since I first set Girart's domain to siege;
I've known no Oliver for all these years;
Now he attacks my host so valiantly
That he has slain before my eyes a Peer
Whom all the gold of Paris would not redeem!   3250
Ride after him, fine youths of high degree,
And capture him and bring him back to me,
But harm him not nor cause him injury!"

When this is said, five score and ten men leave;
The French call out: "Mountjoy, for St. Denis!"   3255
The first in chase is Entelme of Senlis;
He is well armed upon a noble steed,
With coat and helm and a hard, burnished spear;
Before the rest in hot pursuit he speeds —
    Which is his mighty folly!   3260

96

Before the rest the range an archer draws,
Entelme pursues, well armed upon his horse:
"Knights, follow hard!" he calls in a loud voice:
"You take Girart — for Oliver is caught!
If we can take these traitors, one and all,   3265
The whole world's gold will never help their cause,
They will all hang, like robbers foul and false."
Such words aggrieve brave Oliver the more
And he'll not stop, though all his limbs are shorn,
From challenging Entelme with all his force: 3270
He lifts his pike , like a fierce-fighting lord,
And strikes Entelme on his shield's quartered boards;
Beneath the boss he breaks it through and bores
The coat of white, whose mesh and mail are torn;
Inside his ribs he bathes the iron's point;   3275
He spears him well and flings him to the floor;
The helmet's edge he rams into the soil;
He gallops on, like a good fighter ought,
And does not deign to take Entelme's good horse;
But then he turns and rides towards the corpse,   3280
And in reproof he speaks this sentence forth:
"You'll ride no more, you wretched good-for-naught!
Ill-starred you raised your quintain-posts for sport:
A wicked penance you've had to pay for all,
    In worthy Vienne parish!"   3285

97

Towards Vienne rides Oliver forthwith,
When he has felled Entelme and slaughtered him;

Charles sees the deed and almost leaves his wits;
He shows it to his men and then says this:
"Barons, my lords, did you all witness it?   3290
Was there ever a king of my goodwill
Who was misused so foully and paid so ill?
Frenchmen, ride out and do not stop or stint
Till you are sure you have him in your grip!
Fine nephew Roland, capture him for your King!"   3295
When this is said, one hundred turn as bid,
Each one of them a landed count or prince;
Give ear, my lords, God bless you, as I sing
Of the mischance which now befalls and hits
Count Oliver, the wise and strong of limb: 3300
By a rough ditch at the foot of a hill
His lively horse treads awkwardly and trips,
And Oliver falls off beside the ditch;
The Frenchmen come and they surround him quick:
"God," says the count, "fine and majestic King,   3305
Protect your man, and you, brave St. Maurice!"
Ferrant jumps up and he remounts and lifts
His pike aloft, which he grasps by the grip;
The French see him prepared to joust them still:
Ill-starred the lord who charges him full-tilt,   3310
Though he's a count of Burgundy the rich!
Count Oliver sees him and does not flinch:
He grasps his pike and deals him such a hit
He breaks his shield and bursts his hauberk-rings;
Into his ribs he rams the great pike's tip   3315
And throws him down the length that the shaft is;
All Vienne's men leap from the glade they're in:
To help the youth they gallop like the wind,
Girart the strong spurring that horse of his;
Beneath Vienne, in a broad field and big,   3320
The forces meet — Vienne's and the French King's;
Hernaut is there, famed for his fighting skill,
Lord of Biaulande, feared by his enemies;
And that strong vassal's there, young Aymeri;
The youngest there spares elders not a bit,   3325
Nor does the low spare the high, landed prince,
    In this fearsome pitched battle.

98

Count Oliver remounts his destrier,
His shaft in hand, his shield around his neck;
Girart the duke rides up to lend him help;   3330
The range an archer draws before the rest
He moves to strike Bavaria's Naimes:
Upon his shield a mighty blow he sends;
Naimes likewise strikes him with fierce prowess
And both the shafts of their strong spears are cleft;   3335
Their worthy running steeds race on ahead;
At this, behold a fierce melee commence,
And it bids fair to end in grief and death;
Roland the duke seeks out Count Oliver:
"True Emperor," the warrior Roland says: 3340
"Do you observe that armed knight over there
With a green shield of gold bands edge to edge?
He bears a banner in quarters, with a crest
Of a fierce eagle which flies as the flag spreads;
So help me God, that is Count Oliver!   3345
No better knight fights now before Vienne,
    Nor in this entire country!"

99

"Hear me, true Emperor," young Roland says:
"Do you observe that armed knight over there,
Who bears a shield with golden bands inlaid?   3350
That's Oliver, who from Geneva hails,
Son of the feared and fearsome Duke Renier;
Within Vienne there's none more widely famed;
For the gold of two towns I'll not refrain
From matching strength against this lord today!   3355
Then I shall know how fierce he is and brave
And how much to be feared when war is waged."
"For God's sake, no, nephew!" says Charlemagne:
"I'll not allow in combat face to face
The best two knights in Christendom's domain!   3360
If you and he should joust with lances raised,
One of you would be vanquished, that much is plain;
And that one's fame could never rise again."

"Lord, nonetheless," says Roland, obdurate:
"For two towns' gold I will not turn away,   3365
Lest I be given, and earn, a coward's name;
Where seek it hence, if it lies here in wait?
With our spears' iron our merits shall be weighed:
One shall fall short — and so be it, I say."
"Nephew," says Charles, "then go in Lord God's name;   3370
Let His hand see to it you are not slain,
Nor Oliver lose limb or life the same;
May the Lord grant that he shall ride back safe
To his own kin behind the city's gate."
When this is said, young Roland turns in haste;   3375
His golden spurs goad his good destrier
At Oliver with all the speed it may;
The ladies all, meanwhile, have made their way
Out of Vienne to watch the jousting made;
Among them comes fair Aude, the lovely-faced,   3380
Who is a maid of great beauty and grace;
This day she has put on a cloak, a cape
That is quite short but tailored to her shape;
She slips it off her shoulders a short way
Until its hem brushes the meadow-plain;   3385
Lords, will you hear the beauty of this maid?
Upon her head a diadem is placed
Of precious stones which shed a dazzling ray;
Her hair is fair, in ringlets all arranged;
Her eyes are green as a falcon's encaged,   3390
And her face is as fresh of hue and fair
As is the rose picked on a summer's day;
Her hands are white, her fingers full of grace,
Her hips are low and her feet finely shaped;
Her skin is whiter than meadow flowers in May,   3395
With bright blood rising into her cheeks and face;
In Christendom there lives no fairer maid;
Roland sees here and cannot look away!
Deep in his heart he longs for her embrace;
The hardy youth is so held by the maid   3400
That he forgets the joust with Oliver!
He spurs his horse towards fair Aude in haste
And seizes her to carry her away;

For Charles's host and royal tent he makes,
Where he would have all of his will and way;   3405
But the young maid begins to cry and wail:
"Sir Oliver, where are you, brother brave?
Charles's nephew is stealing me away
To the King's host where he will do me shame!
The blemish shall be mine but yours the blame!   3410
May it not please Majestic God, I pray,
That I be used so shamefully this way."
When Oliver hears this, he rides in chase
And, seeing Roland, he calls to him and says:
"Nephew of Charles, for so I hear you named,   3415
Leave my sister alone and show her grace!
Four archbishops shall bless her wedding-day;
Lord Hernaut shall attend, much to be praised,
And Renier of Geneva upon the waves,
And Duke Girart, worthy of so much praise,   3420
And Aymeri, the well-bred and the brave:
From my own hand you may have her that day!"
Roland hears this and flies into a rage:
"Vassal," he says, "give your bravado rein!
I shall take her, whomever this dismays,   3425
To the King's camp — no one shall say me nay!
There I shall have all of my will and way;
If this displeases you, I do not care!"
Says Oliver: "Give your bravado rein!
Your words alone are worthy of great blame;   3430
By that same Saint whom we should seek in praise,
If someone else had boasted in this vein,
I would have said: 'You are a lying knave!';
But if, in truth, you would abduct this maid,
Then you shall have a heavy price to pay: 3435
A joust with me — if you can dare to wait!"
Roland replies: "I gladly grant the same;
Ride over there and give me jousting-space!"
Says Oliver: "Most gladly I'll obey;
You are a duke, I am a count proclaimed;   3440
This joust of ours is justly meant and made,
For both of us are princes of our states."
With spurs of gold they goad their destriers,

Against their breast their worthy shields embraced;
With all the speed their lively steeds can make   3445
They charge each other across the meadow-plain;
Great blows they swap upon their shields ornate,
And their nielloed spears splinter and break;
Their coats are strong, they do not rip the mail,
And neither falls as their steeds pass at pace;   3450
When Oliver sees this, he is enraged
That in the joust Roland remains unscathed;
He draws his sword, with its bright, shining blade,
And deals his jeweled helm a blow so great
That stones and floral emblems are struck away   3455
And the good helm is crushed and cracked in twain;
The mighty blow stuns Roland, and I'd say
That had the Lord not shown His saving grace,
And had the coif-cap on his white coat been frail,
This blow would have sent Roland into his grave;   3460
His horse falls down beneath the blow's great weight,
And when it stands, it bolts off in escape;
Roland's borne off some three acres away,
Not knowing where the horse's flight is aimed,
Whether Vienne, whether to Charlemagne!   3465
Thus Oliver the brave rescues and saves
His sister Aude, the lovely fair-faced maid,
      In joust by Vienne city.

100

Roland the duke, when he comes to his senses,
Is filled with rage and flushes with displeasure   3470
At the great blow which Count Oliver dealt him:
Never before had Roland been so bested!
The war-horse bolts back to the host of Frenchmen
And Charlemagne comes forth to meet his nephew;
From Roland's head he lifts the broken helmet   3475
And sighs for joy to see him hale and healthy:
"Nephew," he says, "I was afraid and fretting
Lest you were slain and lain upon the meadow;
But by the Saint whom God strengthens, I tell you,
Girart has angered me enough already!   3480

If I can capture him, I'll hang the felon
    In front of all Vienne."

101

King Charlemagne is mightily aggrieved
At Oliver for all the woe he's wreaked;
But then behold a well-armed knight appear,   3485
A count of Berry and born in Burgundy;
A godson of the King and kin is he;
One hundred knights are in his power to lead,
For his prowess and his own pride's increase;
He drops the reins and lets the horse run free   3490
To strike in joust Count Oliver's strong shield;
Beneath the boss he drills so big a breach
A sparrow-hawk could pass through it with ease!
When Oliver sees this, his rage is deep;
He swears an oath with all the hate he feels,   3495
By Vienne's saint, the valiant Maurice,
That he'll pay dearly for it before he leaves!
Garin brings forth to him a solid spear;
With four gold nails a flag's fixed to its peak;
He arms himself to joust Lanbert — but see   3500
The lovely Aude running across the field!
She lifts her mantle's hem above her feet;
As it slips down, her shoulders are revealed;
Between both ranks she hails Lanbert in speech;
"My lords, look there!" each baron says to each: 3505
"Have you beheld a woman as fair as she?
He who takes her to be his wife and peer,
Can bless the hour that he was born, indeed!"
The fair maid does not halt but runs to seize
Lanbert the count by his gold-banded shield;   3510
She draws it near and he stoops down to hear
As the young maid makes him this speech and plea:
"Fine knight, curb your desire for jousting here
With Oliver, my brother brave and dear!
Surrender and enter Vienne with me!   3515
Your bondage shall be light: you will be free
To come and go in my rooms as you please,

Where we can share in laughter and in glee;
And if you wish I shall bring there and leave
A lovely maid of high birth and degree;   3520
You may enjoy your will with her at ease;
No one shall treat her hence with less esteem;
For love of you she shall be wed in brief."
"Fair one," he says, "let all this talking be!
Though all my limbs were shorn, I'd not agree!   3525
I would be seen as cowardly and weak,
And my fine kin would hold my honor cheap,
If a young maid wrought my captivity!
With lance's steel young men are meant to meet,
Where one of them is forced to own defeat!"   3530
"My lord," she says, "then my lips shall be sealed;
If you should fail, no blame shall fall to me!"
And she steps back to see the joust proceed;
Lanbert the count is a strong knight indeed;
He brandishes his heavy-headed spear   3535
And with his spurs of gold he goads his steed
At Oliver and deals his golden shield
A blow which bursts the boards and bores between;
His hauberk's strong, none of its mail is breached,
And not to fall shows a fierce lord beneath!   3540
Now Oliver returns the blow and deals
A mighty blow which holes Lanbert's own shield:
Upon his breast he bores so lustily
That, legs aloft, he flings him on the field;
Count Oliver pursues him, sword unsheathed,   3545
And would have slain and slaughtered him in brief,
When Lanbert cries aloud: "Spare me, brave peer!
Here is my sword: your prisoner, I yield!
Take me into Vienne and render me
To Duke Girart, your uncle and your liege!   3550
High ransom for my life you may receive:
Four pack-mules piled with gold and silver each,
One hundred jeweled helms and hauberks sleek,
One hundred pikes and richly banded shields,
One hundred palfreys and well-rested war-steeds,   3555
And bears and hounds and leopards on the leash,
And wealth as well, if such contents your need,

For my own riches are very great indeed."
Says Oliver: "You'll be well held for these!
In Vienne town you will be well received: 3560
Before two months we shall not let you leave!
Girart my uncle will thank me much indeed
For bringing him a guest of such degree!"
He grasps him now by his helm's nasal-piece
And, hailing twenty among his knights, he speaks: 3565
"Lead off this lord to the good town for me!"
And so they do, at Oliver's decree;
They wend their way within the bailey's reach;
When Charles sees this, he almost bursts for grief,
    And shows it to his liegemen.   3570

102

"Look there, my lords," says fierce-faced Charlemagne:
"Count Girart's men have led Lanbert away;
He is my godson, I tell you in all faith;
I greatly fear that he will now be slain;
Ride after him, my worthy knights well-raised,   3575
Before he's brought inside the castle gates!
If we seize one of them, with Lord God's aid,
I could win back Sir Lanbert in exchange."
At this five score and ten spur off in haste:
"Mountjoy for St.Denis!" the French exclaim: 3580
"The flag of St. Maurice!" Vienne's men say:
"Hernaut and Aymeri!" shout Biaulande's brave:
"Geneva!" well-bred Oliver proclaims;
The Vienne knights are bold of heart this day;
Upon the French in force they turn their reins;   3585
My lords, behold a fearsome fight engaged!
The fragments fly as pikes and lances break
And solid shields are holed and split in twain
And burnished helms of green are hit away;
They hack and hew with shining steel-edged blades,   3590
And in the press, at the heart of the fray,
Stands Oliver, the count and marquis brave;
Without God's help, Who on the cross was laid,
Ere evening comes he'll need his comrades' aid!

He looks to ground and sees a bright spear lain   3595
Where a dead knight has fallen to his fate;
So he stoops down and seizes it again,
Prepared to joust as bravely as he may;
The French see him in all his strength and rage,
Cursed if there's one prepared to face him, save   3600
One solitary knight, a baron brave
From Brittany, a count of high estate:
When Oliver sees him, his blow is great:
He splits his shield and slits the hauberk's chains;
Right through the ribs he runs the lance's blade   3605
And rams his helmet's rim into the plain:
"Vienne!" he cries, "God and St. Maurice, aid!
I'm Oliver, no friend of yours, sir knave!"
He looks around and sees Ogier the Dane:
Upon Flori he rides in fierce array;   3610
When Oliver sees this, the count heads straight
To joust with him, preparing on the way;
King Charles looks on and to Roland he says:
"Behold, fine nephew, by St. Rémy I swear
You'll see a joust whose like was never made!   3615
By Lord God Jesus Christ, who shall prevail?"
Roland replies: "Lord Oliver, I'll wage!
I've never seen his like in all my days
For harassing his mortal foe with hate!"
"Ah God, protect my knight!" says Charlemagne: 3620
"Spare him from death and agony and pain,
And save brave Oliver from the same fate:
Let him return alive and whole and hale
Within Vienne, whence he among us came!"
Now Oliver is seen by Duke Ogier,   3625
Who lifts aloft his burnished spear and aims
At his curved shield, and a great blow he lays
Beneath the boss, which smites the boards away;
His hauberk's strong, the chain-mail doesn't break,
And not to fall shows a fierce lord and brave;   3630
Now Oliver strikes Ogier in like vein
Upon his shield and splits it through the grain;
Upon his breast the lance-blow is so great
That down the horse's rump he fells the Dane!

His helmet's rim goes sticking in the plain!   3635
Count Oliver is fierce and fast — he takes
The horse from which he has just felled Ogier;
He looks to right and sees a youth whose name
Is Poinçonet, from his own land and state;
One month had yet to run its span of days   3640
Since Lord Girart had dubbed this Poinçonet;
Says Oliver to him: "Friend, come here, pray:
Look! I give you this noble destrier;
By force of arms I've captured it and claimed;
Go ride it back whence you came forth this day."   3645
"My lord, much thanks indeed," the young knight says;
Alas, my lords, that he once grasped the reins —
He was cut down because of it and slain;
How great a hue and cry the Frenchmen raise,
When Ogier's Arab steed is lost this way;   3650
The Vienne knights rush homeward to the gates;
Count Roland rides in anger and enraged
Along the walls and sees young Poinçonet
As he rides back the noble destrier
Which was the powerful, worthy Duke Ogier's;   3655
He spurs his steed and lifts his lance straightway;
With all his strength he strikes young Poinçonet
On his curved shield and a great blow he lays
Beneath the boss which smites the boards away;
He rips apart and wrecks the hauberk's mail   3660
And through his ribs he rams the lance's blade;
He spears him well and fells him on the plain;
Roland seizes the horse by both its reins
And leads it back to Ogier the good Dane;
The Vienne knights ride back inside the gates,   3665
Which then are closed and the draw-bridge is raised;
Upon an ancient wall fair Aude awaits;
She sees Roland and in a loud voice says:
"Vassal, your spear has served us ill today!
One of our knights lies slaughtered by your rage;   3670
If Lord Girart and my brother had stayed,
You'd not have dared to touch good Poinçonet
For all the gold that Paris town contains."
Roland hears this reproof and bows his face;

The French depart as daylight starts to fade,   3675
Each to his tent whence earlier he came;
Back to his tent turns fierce-faced Charlemagne,
While in Vienne Marquis Girart remains;
Within a porch to Lord St. Maurice raised
They strip the arms from Berry's Count Lanbert;   3680
Girart steps up, the duke of royal rate,
And Lanbert hands to him his burnished blade
And his own self to his mercy and grace;
The burnished helm is lifted from his face,
And from his back the coat of triple mail;   3685
In just a tunic of samite silk he waits;
His skin is bruised where the hauberk has chafed;
Among the others he bears a captive's air,
But he is not forgotten by Aude the fair:
About his neck a rich mantle she drapes,   3690
And then, by the right hand, leads him away,
Climbing the steps to Vienne's hall of state;
Upon a cushion she bids him take his place
Beside her there, and then the fair maid says:
"Lanbert, my lord, do not be too dismayed!   3695
For love of God, Who never lies or fails,
Know that Girart is a knight who is brave
And nobly bred to valor and high grace,
Rich in his birth and in his friends the same;
He will not seek, I swear to you in faith,   3700
A ransom which shall leave you poor, when paid."
"Lady, much thanks for these kind words," he says:
"No need of yours, however far away,
That I shall know of, while I am whole and hale,
Shall not be met with two thousand men's aid,   3705
In shining arms on Arab destriers!"
"My lord, much thanks for these kind words," she says;
They ask for water, then sit at tables laid,
    To dine in Vienne palace.

103

They ask for water and then they sit to eat;   3710
Brave Oliver and Girart take their seats

With Sir Hernaut of Biaulande on the sea
And all their lords of most praiseworthy feats;
Lanbert the count sits next to Aude the sweet,
While further down sit other knights and peers;   3715
I will not strive to tell you of their feast:
The hungry man could well content his need;
But Sir Lanbert can eat nothing, it seems!
Girart the duke calls out to him and speaks:
"My lord Lanbert, take food and drink at least: 3720
You cannot have all that your eyes can see!"
Lanbert replies: "Lord, do you know, indeed?
You have said this, I think, for your own niece;
Yet she's a maid and I am young in years;
Nor should my birth be placed against my plea;   3725
Neither my lands or riches are so mean
That I should fear to marry such as she —
And if not her, there's many a woman here,
And none as good as God shall choose for me!"
Lord Girart says: "Let all this talking be!   3730
There's something else that I would have you hear:
If you can bring great Charles and me to peace,
I shall release you before tomorrow eve,
For hostages, if you deliver these."
Lanbert replies: "Much thanks for this reprieve;   3735
Of all my wealth you may have what you please;
Thirty pack-mules with riches shall be heaped,
And, if you wish, this number I'll increase,
For my own wealth is great enough indeed."
Count Oliver looks hard, when this he hears;   3740
He calls Girart aside, quite quietly,
To speak with him so none may overhear:
"My lord Girart," says Oliver the fierce:
"Have you before heard such a captive's speech?
Do not accept, I urge you, the least piece   3745
Of all the wealth of which you hear him speak:
Free him and Charles will make a greater peace;
If he does not, his honor will be cheap."
Girart hears this and shakes his brow and beard:
"Nephew," he says, "I'll do as you decree,   3750
And deal exactly as you say I should deal!"

When all have had their fill of meat and mead,
Servants and squires move up and cloths are cleared;
With no delay the knights straightway all leave
For their own lodging-place to rest and sleep; 3755
Girart the duke does not forget Lanbert;
Within the hall a bed's installed, complete
With costly cushions and rugs from overseas;
They bid Lanbert to slumber there in peace;
The maiden Aude comes up to him and speaks: 3760
"My lord Lanbert, be of good heart and cheer;
For lord God's sake do not dismay or fear;
Girart the duke is a fine knight indeed,
A noble vassal and valiant in the field,
And rich alike in wealth and property; 3765
He will not seek a ransom which brings you grief."
"Fair one," he says, "I do thank you indeed;
You have brought me much comfort and much ease;
I pledge to you in turn my loyalty;
However far away, if you're in need, 3770
I'll lead three thousand knights to your relief."
"My lord, I thank you much for this," says she;
At this she turns back to her room to sleep;
Girart the duke does not forget Lanbert;
Within the hall he sets a bed complete 3775
With fourteen candles to light his head and feet;
Ten knights are dressed and armed in all their gear
To guard Lanbert all of the hours he sleeps,
Until the morn and the dawn light appears,
So that he may in no way rise and leave; 3780
When morning comes and they hear the bells peal,
Girart the duke and all his men of liege,
With Oliver and Lanbert, brave of breed,
Lady Guibourc and lovely Aude the sweet,
Move off to Mass, which all attend and hear; 3785
When this is said and the last prayer is preached,
They leave the church and to the hall proceed;
At the high table there see Girart lean —
    The lord of Vienne city!

104

Lord Girart leaves the church when Mass is said;   3790
Back in the hall at his high seat he rests;
Lanbert of Berry comes to address him then:
"My lord Girart," the warrior Lanbert says:
"What counsel have you taken upon my head?
What fee shall set me free, what hostages?   3795
From Charles's host the ransom shall be sent
By high-born knights who are esteemed the best."
Says Oliver: "You speak of foolishness,
For by the Saint whom knights seek to address,
For all the gold that's in Montpellier   3800
We do not wish for one coin of your wealth;
Though you serve Charles, the fierce-faced Emperor,
No noble man should censure your prowess;
For every knight should serve his lord's behest,
Since from his liege he holds his fief or realm;   3805
He must oblige, when his liege-lord needs help,
With shining arms and iron of cutting edge —
Unless it be to rob churches and vex
The lowly poor and cause them more distress:
No man should wage a war with God Himself,   3810
For he would fall before he'd gone one step."
"You are no craven soul," replies Lanbert:
"How wise he was who taught your heart so well!"
"Fine sister Aude," says Count Oliver next:
"The time has come for Lanbert to go hence;   3815
And what is more, he should be recompensed
By some rich gift or cloth of great expense
To pride himself upon with the King's men."
"My lord," she says, "I readily assent;
I have, I think, an item to present,   3820
Which has no peer from here to Montpellier,
    In king or count's possession."

105

The maiden Aude is of high birth and sense;
Down from the hall with every haste she steps
Into her room without delay or let;   3825

The worthy maid, inside, goes to a chest
Where many a flag of silken cloth is kept;
She seizes forth the richest one of them:
From edge to edge it shines with precious gems
And bands of finest gold and silver threads;   3830
Back to the hall fair Aude the maiden heads;
She bears the flag within the hall and then
She lays it out before the knight Lanbert;
How wondrously the eyes of all are held
By its bright hue, of many colors blent!   3835
In truth, not one of the Apostles Twelve
You would not find to be depicted there,
And in fine gold are to be found as well
The face and form of lovely Aude herself;
No man who bears that flag into the press   3840
Need fear the might or pride of other men
Nor any evil plot planned for his death;
The lovely Aude gives this to Sir Lanbert,
Who, taking it, gives thanks for this largesse;
To a long shaft he clips the banner then   3845
And climbs aloft the great tower of Vienne;
There he displays the flag to all the French;
The flag unfurls from a high window's ledge
And Charles's host looks up and sees it well;
Roland does too and all his color ebbs;   3850
He points it out to all his men and says:
"Behold Lanbert, my worthy honored friends!
He and fair Aude have talked of peace in there,
And Count Lanbert has been well recompensed;
Without a sword he has pierced my own flesh!   3855
If Duke Girart has given him such wealth,
      Then our fighting is finished."

106

Girart the warrior says: "Oliver, nephew,
On my behalf, equip Lanbert of Berry:
Return to him his clothes, his horse and weapons   3860
So that his loss amounts to not one penny

Of all the wealth with which he was attended;
Give back to him each one of his possessions
And give him more, if he deigns to accept them."
Count Oliver replies: "My lord, with pleasure."   3865
Without delay they hasten off to fetch him
His noble robes and dearest gear directly;
In a white coat of double weave they dress him
And then lace on his green and golden helmet;
Girart holds forth his sword of steel well-tempered,   3870
Which Oliver against his left hip tethers;
The squires lead forth his lithe and lively destrier
And Lanbert mounts the stirrup on the left side;
Around his neck a quartered shield is settled
And then a strong and cutting spear's presented   3875
To which they have attached the flag already
Given by Aude, of fierce and fine complexion:
"My lord Lanbert," Girart the warrior tells him:
"I free you for no gold or the least penny!
And with you goes dear Oliver, my nephew;   3880
I pray you, in God's name, the Lord of Heaven,
Allow no shame or vicious deed to vex him."
Lanbert replies: "This plea needs no requesting,
For, by the Lord Who governs all in Heaven,
There is no man so fierce among the Frenchmen   3885
Whom, if he tries to be a fool or felon,
I will not force to stay his hand directly —
If he does not, he shall dearly regret it;
Unless it is the King of France himself, or
The warrior Sir Roland, his own nephew —   3890
These two alone I would not dare to censure."
Count Oliver moves off now to make ready;
In a white coat of double weave he dresses,
On top of which he then has tightly tethered
A costly tunic cut to his size and measure;   3895
Around his neck a rich mantle he settles,
Then mounts the stirrups of his fleet-footed destrier;
Out of the town the two knights ride together
Without delay until they reach the Frenchmen,
     To tell them of their news.   3900

107

When lovely Aude sees her dear brother leave,
Most tenderly the maiden starts to weep:
"Oliver, lord," the fair-faced maiden speaks:
"I pray to God the Lord, our Heavenly Liege,
Who in the Virgin's womb deigned once to be,   3905
And on the Cross's boards did deign to bleed,
To guard your life from death or injury;
I pray that Charles may not bring you to grief,
Neither Sir Roland, who is much to be feared."
She calls Garin, his young squire, to appear: 3910
"My friend," she says, "pay careful heed to me:
Go gather up your master's arms and gear
And with them all ride hard upon his heels,
So he may have them close, if there is need;
So help me God, a good reward you'll reap!"   3915
"Just as you wish, my fair lady," says he,
And takes the arms and sets off with all speed;
To the French camp he comes so stealthily
And hides beneath a well-branched, leafy tree,
That no man there of mother born to breathe   3920
    Sees him in the King's army.

108

Beneath a tree squire Garin lies in wait;
He holds the arms of brave Count Oliver:
If he's in need, he'll bring them forth straightway;
Before the tent of fierce-faced Charlemagne   3925
Lanbert of Berry dismounts his destrier,
Together with the marquis Oliver,
And plants his spear before the entrance-way
Like a fine knight who is much to be praised;
The worthy flag flies in the wind and waves,   3930
Which he was given by Aude the fierce of face;
The valiant knights behold it there and gaze —
But none as much as Lord Roland the brave;
He points it out to Count Manesier;
"Who is this knight?" each to the other says;   3935
Roland replies: "Lanbert of Berry state;

With brave Girart his own peace he has made,
And he has met with Aude the fierce of face,
And from my love he has led her astray!"
"Have you then seen, my lord," says Manesier: 3940
"The maiden Aude, who is much to be praised?"
"Indeed I have, I'll not conceal the same;
When I rode forth to joust on Vienne's plain,
Beneath the walls I went in sport that day;
I seized the maid on my swift destrier   3945
And would, without a risk, have made away,
When Oliver, her brother, up and came,
And rescued her with his burnished steel blade."
"Roland, my lord," says Count Manesier:
"I will not hide that Aude is a fair maid;   3950
I know of none more to be prized and praised."
When this is said, both of those knights make haste
Inside the tent of Emperor Charlemagne;
The French all say: "What is this fine knight's name,
Who has brought back Lanbert of Berry safe?"   3955
Says one who knows: "He is Count Oliver,
He who began the fight by our quintain,
And who still kills fine knights of ours each day;
If we attend him not, we shall be shamed!"
Ten score and more run to his stirrup's aid,   3960
But squire Garin seizes the destrier,
Son of Achart of Valley Rivier,
Who is his cousin whose love for him is great;
Up to one hundred knights of the best rate
Among the French, behold now, as in train   3965
They lead Girart's envoy to Charlemagne;
The tent fills up with princes of high sway,
Who come to hear what Oliver will say;
Before the King, fierce-visaged Charles the great,
    He comes to speak his message.   3970

109

Before King Charles, the Lord of St. Denis,
The marquis Oliver comes striding in;
He frees the clasp from his gray cloak and rich

And from his back the young lord loosens it —
He lets it fall, not caring who assists;   3975
Then he kneels down before great Charles the King
And greets the fierce-faced Emperor with this:
"May God, Who pardoned Longinus his sin,
Safeguard King Charles, the Lord of St. Denis,
And may he save Sir Girart the marquis,   3980
My own dear uncle, the strong lord that he is!
True Emperor, hear what I seek and bring:
Girart the duke, who was your friend ere this,
Returns to you Lanbert, of ransom quit;
For all the gold from here to fair Paris   3985
He'll not hold him four days against your will!
For Girart is your man by oath and kiss
And holds his land from you and all that's his;
Take care, fine king, that you commit no ill
Whereby Girart becomes your enemy!   3990
Return to France, to Rheims or to Paris!
Marquis Girart will follow you forthwith
And one thousand fine knights with him he'll bring:
Such is the sum that this land owes to him;
And he will serve you there as you best wish."   3995
When Charles hears this, he drops his cheek and chin
And then replies, yet most pensively still:
"What is your name, my proud and handsome prince?"
The youth replies: "My name is Oliver."
Fierce Charles replies: "I well believe it is;   4000
Speak all your speech; use all your skill and wit,
And then return whence you have come with it!"
The well-bred count replies: "My lord, I will:
But lift your head and mark my looks and lips!
I'll tell you all that I do know and think;   4005
    No man alive shall stop me."

110

"True Emperor," Count Oliver repeats:
"I give you back Lanbert, of ransom free;
He has not lost his weapons or his steed,
Nor anything that's worth a penny-piece;   4010

Girart, my uncle, has sent me with him here;
I will not hide, he charges you through me
That you oppose him here most wrongfully
And waste his realm and devastate his fiefs;
He bids you to return to France the sweet;   4015
Brave Girart will go with you when you leave;
Two thousand knights shall keep him company
And he shall serve you well and willingly,
And any wrong be ready to redeem."
"Vassal," says Charles, "he has much angered me: 4020
Without revenge I shall be filled with grief,
For wondrous large is the siege-host I lead
And we have laid this siege for seven years,
Which you ask me to lift so easily;
By the Lord God to Whom our prayers should reach,   4025
I tell you straight, before ever I'll leave,
Girart the brave shall know he's met defeat:
And he shall come before me on his knees,
In a hair-shirt, unshod, to cry for peace;
Around his neck he'll clutch the stirrups each   4030
Tied to the saddle of some poor sumpter-beast."
Says Oliver: "Sire, that will never be,
For Lord Girart is very proud and fierce,
      And of a powerful family."

111

Count Oliver, the brave and wise, speaks forth: 4035
"Listen to me awhile, true Emperor!
So help me God in majesty adored,
I shall tell you my message and my thoughts
From start to finish, for I would have it all
Heard and well known by these fine knights of yours: 4040
Vienne was my grandfather's — you know it, lord,
And, proven truth, his grandfather's before;
My grandfather was long-bearded Beuvon,
Who ruled this realm for five score years and more;
No King of France ever opposed his law;   4045
It seems to me that you are most at fault
To seek land that is my uncle's of yore;

If you succeed, you are the criminal;
And by the Saint in Nero's field besought,
In holy Rome where his name is adored,   4050
Before you are installed in Vienne's walls,
Before you have secured its strongest fort,
I shall set sail across the sea to call
Upon one of my uncle's, a monarch called
King Afloaires, a fearsome warrior;   4055
No man alive will make him fail my cause;
He will arm men some twenty thousand score
And I shall lead them here to fight this war;
I tell you truly, I shall lead forth all four
Of Garin's sons, with all their fearsome force;   4060
When all these noble men lend their support,
Some forty thousand knights in rank shall form;
And we shall ride in a relentless course
From here to France astride our steeds of war;
We shall not leave one town of yours unspoilt;   4065
No tower of stone, no castle or rich fort
Shall be left standing; each one of them shall fall!"
"Madman, you boast too much!" the King retorts:
"I do not care two shelled eggs for your vaunts!"
When this is said, just as you've heard it, lords,   4070
Inside the tent strides Roland, who is joined
By the Twelve Peers, in pairs appearing all;
Beside the King Roland leans on the boards;
What stinging words shall now be heard, my lords,
Whereby Roland's and Oliver's proud swords   4075
    Shall clash on Vienne's island.

112

Roland the valiant-visaged fighter says:
"True Emperor, this vassal's gall is great,
To throw these taunts directly in your face!
Go, Oliver! Your preaching is insane!   4080
Can you deny, brag wildly as you may,
That Duke Girart has not broken the faith
Which he has pledged to his king Charlemagne?"
Says Oliver: "You have no proof to lay!

Please God, the Son of the blest Virgin Maid,   4085
That you would pledge your own word right away,
That in the morning, as soon as dawn shall break,
You'll come alone to the isle on the lake
Beneath Vienne, the worthy town well-graced,
Armed and astride your Syrian destrier;   4090
There we shall fight with our sharp, burnished blades,
I for Girart, of visage bright and brave,
You for King Charles, whose beard is gray with age."
Roland hears this, and his cheeks burn in shame
    For Charles's knights and barons.   4095

113

"Sir Oliver," Roland the brave replies:
"How has Girart not broken faith and lied
To Charlemagne, who is his king by right,
To whom he pledged his loyalty and life?
He has no rights to properties and shires,   4100
To towns and towers or castles fortified!
He should escape and dwell in foreign climes
Beyond the sea among the Pagan tribes."
"Roland, my lord," the valiant Lanbert cries:
"You are much in the wrong, so help me Christ!   4105
Girart the duke is a most worthy knight,
A noble vassal and brave in battle's strife;
And Oliver is a fine knight alike;
If you had been down in the field erstwhile,
You would not think of him as otherwise."   4110
Says Oliver: "Say nothing more, sir knight;
Roland the count speaks much, but I surmise
That doing more is far from his desire!
Roland, my lord, heed well these words of mine:
Are you a woman, to argue all the time?   4115
Pledge me your word, on your faith as a knight,
That in the morning, when the sun starts to rise,
Beneath Vienne you will come to the isle,
Bringing no other of mother born to life,
Except the horse on which you're armed to fight;   4120
And we shall fight with good swords at our side,

I for Girart, the noblest duke alive,
And you for Charles, who is a king by right;
Since we shall fight alone, God shall decide
Who gains the verdict and honor, you or I."   4125
Roland hears this and anger fills his mind;
He moves to strike him there, but thinks in time
That, if he did, it would be thought a crime:
An envoy should be let to speak his mind;
So, thinking thus, Roland controls his pride,   4130
Not wishing blame to fall upon his side;
He draws his glove with golden bands incised,
Comes to the King and, seen by every eye,
He proffers it in vow that he will fight
With Oliver, who is a valiant knight;   4135
Beneath Vienne on the expanse of isle
They pledge that both in armor shall arrive
    To fight in single combat.

114

Lords, you have heard of the agreement sworn
Before the King of mighty France and all   4140
His barons there and all his knights and lords;
The pledges and the covenant set forth
That Roland claims rich Vienne city for
King Charlemagne, whose beard and hair are hoar,
But Oliver, the valiant-visaged lord,   4145
Defends Girart with his well-burnished sword,
Of treachery to Charles in deed or thought:
And if he wins in combat to be fought
Against Duke Roland of bravery galore,
Then the French force will journey home once more   4150
And make no claim upon Vienne henceforth;
And if Lord Oliver loses and falls,
Then Duke Girart, the worthy, mighty lord,
Will leave Vienne, the wealthy and strong-walled,
And keep nothing of it worth the least coin;   4155
    But will return to Puglia.

115

Count Oliver speaks on: "So help me Jesus,
The righteous God, yours is the wrong and treason
And haughty pride, and I shall not conceal it,
If you challenge Vienne, intent to seize it   4160
And chase Girart away and make him leave here;
But if Lord God, Who judges all, so pleases,
You shall not take one penny-piece from Girart,
While I may fight with my good horse beneath me!
I trust so much in God to judge the evil,   4165
That if Roland and I must fight between us,
I am quite sure I shall disprove and beat him —
If Lord God in His mercy will help and heed me;
But truly, Sire, once more I do beseech you:
Put off this fight which we have both agreed to,   4170
By putting off the siege of this great siege-host
And going back to sweet France with your legion;
I and Girart, the uncle I love dearly,
Will follow you most willingly, believe me,
And serve King Charlemagne the fierce of feature   4175
In every need, as our true, rightful liege-lord;
If you do not, by the bones of St. Riquier,
Never again shall I strive to entreat you,
But to defy you — and I shall not conceal it,
In Lord God's name, Who can well teach you meekness   4180
And stoop your proud and arrogant demeanor!"
Roland hears this and thinks he'll lose all reason,
Moving to strike him, but not daring to either!
The other Peers, who see his anger seething,
Grasp his right arm to hold him back and lead him   4185
To his own tent to let him rest and sleep there;
Before the King stands Oliver, unyielding,
Like a brave knight defending what he believes in
    Before all Charles's lords.

116

Hernaut of Mongençon gets to his feet;   4190
He lifts his voice and like a villain speaks:
"True Emperor, my lord, give me your ear!

By blessèd Simon's bones, if you heed me,
This wretch should hang upon the gallows-tree!
Then, with no more delay, when dawn appears,   4195
Let us assault this town Vienne and seize
Lord Girart forth and force him then to yield;
He has no force which we cannot defeat;
When he is caught, allow no ransom fee
    To free him from your justice!"   4200

117

When Oliver hears his life threatened so
With hanging as a thief or common rogue,
And when he hears alike the menace thrown
To thrust Girart out of the lands he owns,
He thinks he'll go insane with rage and woe!   4205
Without revenge he'll hold his honor low,
And so he moves towards the wretch Hernaut;
Step after step like a fierce lord he goes
And by the hair he hauls the villain close;
Hernaut drops down with the force of the hold   4210
And Oliver's strong fist lands such a blow
Upon his neck it breaks the collar-bone;
Out of his mouth the blood bursts forth and flows
As on the ground he lays the villain cold;
When Aimart sees his wounded uncle roll   4215
Upon the ground and hears him moan and groan,
You can be sure that hatred fills his soul;
In vicious haste for Oliver he goes
And by the temple-hairs he hauls him close;
The count drops down with the force of the hold: 4220
"God!" says Lanbert, "My help may be too slow!"
He draws his sword with all the haste he knows
And strikes Aimart, not holding back the stroke:
He hews his head — beside the King it rolls —
And flings him dead by his uncle Hernaut;   4225
When Charles sees this, his anger is full-blown;
He cries aloud: "Knights, take these two in hold!
And if they move, then cut both of their throats!
    For they have shamed me greatly."

118

"True Emperor," the brave Lanbert retorts: 4230
"So help me God, the shame and wrong are yours!
Cursed be the court where one dares not speak forth
One's honest thoughts or message one has brought!
Cursed be the king who will not hear such thoughts!
You know full well, my lord, I had been caught   4235
Before Vienne, where I had gone and fought
With Oliver, who is now in your court;
I was led off inside Vienne by force,
But I was served and treated with great warmth;
Never in France, even where I was born,   4240
Was I received more nobly than in their ward;
Now I'm released so freely by Girart
That I've not lost in all two denier coins!
I have come back, as you have seen, my lord,
On the same horse that I had led before,   4245
And with my arms and armor all restored;
I was brought back by the wise Oliver,
Whose safety I should surely answer for!
For his goodwill he's earned a poor reward,
Held up straightway to insult and to scorn   4250
By all these rogues, God curse them one and all!
If I helped him, it was no crime or fault!"
When this is said, he cries with ringing voice:
"You knights of mine, where have you gone, my lords?"
Five hundred cry: "We are here at your call,   4255
Equipped and armed with our well-burnished swords."
The count replies: "Praise be to God the Lord!
Out of my lands I have led you all forth;
I urge you now, who love me as your lord,
And hold your fiefs and lands from me in law,   4260
That in my need you do not serve me false,
Nor Oliver, who stands before you all
As he who set me free from Vienne's fort."
They all respond: "You doubt our faith for naught!
We shall not fail you, though all our limbs be shorn!"   4265
When they say this, no Frenchman there henceforth
Dares move against Lanbert or vex him more;
     And so the madness lessens.

119

When Oliver sees all the French step near him,
He does not think that he will leave there breathing!   4270
The press is thick with noble knights and liegemen,
And they move up, surrounding him to seize him;
They rip aside his samite silken bliaut
And then the gray and rich pelisse beneath it;
The count dismays and fills with rage to feel it;   4275
He moves across and grasps a pole that leans there,
By which the tent is held aloft and even;
He rips it from its spot, his anger seething,
And the ropes snap and send to ground the sheeting;
Fine Oliver picks up the pole and wields it;   4280
The man he strikes knows that his end is near him!
Lanbert looks on and calls so he may hear him:
"Brave Marquis Oliver, leave, I beseech you!
I can no longer be certain of your freedom!
For all the gold in Paris I would not see you   4285
Killed or ill-used or injured here by treason!"
Says Oliver: "Much thanks for this release, lord!"
And he turns round, not asking leave but leaving
The tent with all his enemies still reeling!
Garin the squire, who is his friend, believe me,   4290
Has made quite sure that his good horse will be there;
Straight from the ground he leaps into its seat there,
But does not fail to use the stirrups either —
His noble horse begins straightway to feel them!
Throughout the host Count Oliver rides keenly: 4295
To save his life he is obliged to flee them;
As he looks to his right beneath the trees there
He sees the squire whom Aude had sent to meet him;
He spurs his horse and turns that way to greet him;
And the good youth is unafraid and eager   4300
To render him the fine armor he's needing,
Which he puts on like a knight of good breeding:
Upon his back the coat of triple weaving
And on his head the helmet green and gleaming;
He girds the sword, whose blade is burnished sleekly,   4305
And then remounts his worthy horse, while seizing
A solid pike of burnish rich and recent,

Held out to him by the good squire who serves him;
And when he is equipped and armed completely,
He's keen to joust with any foe appearing! 4310
He rides downhill and out into a clearing,
As does his squire, who is both fair and fearless;
See then, my lords, Sir Girart riding fiercely
With Hernaut of Biaulande, of fearsome feature,
And Aymeri and Renier of Geneva; 4315
Girart the duke calls loudly, when he sees him:
"How have you fared, fine friend and nephew dearest?"
"Badly, my lord; I pledge you most sincerely,
I did repeat your message loud and clearly
For Charles the King of St. Denis to hear it, 4320
Together with all of his knights and peerage;
Roland and I shall fight this war between us:
Before the King I pledged that I would meet him."
Girart replies: "Lord God, the King of Heaven,
Assist our cause with Your grace, I entreat you! 4325
Nephew, have you not sought or wrought agreement
Or other peace among the French and me here?"
"By St. Maurice, I've not, my lord, believe me;
They've chased me off — look up, my lord, and see them!
Let us turn back, for God and for Lord Jesus, 4330
And welcome them like knights of noble breeding."
Girart replies: "I grant your wish most freely!"
When this is said, they spur those steeds beneath them,
With bucklers pressed against their breasts to shield them;
They meet the French who, armed to fight, receive them; 4335
They drop the reins of their good steeds to speed them;
Without delay, as fast as they can reach them,
They strike their curving shields with their sharp spearpoints;
The fight is fierce and full of zeal and feeling;
Lances are split as shields are hit and beaten, 4340
And coats of mail are reft and cleft to pieces
As knights are felled from their Arabian steeds there;
Before the rest, see Aymeri appearing
To strike a Frank upon his gray-brown shield there!
Beneath the boss he breaks the boards completely: 4345
The hauberk's strong, the mail parts not nor pierces,
Though from his Arab steed he sends him reeling:

"Vienne and St. Maurice!" he cries, "Strike each one
And all of you like knights of worthy breeding!"
And so they do, most valiantly and keenly,   4350
Though Aymeri among them all is peerless!
Back to their tents they fight the French and seek them
And lay them low and slay them on the field there!
Marquis Girart comes to the tents and sees there
Fine steeds galore and weapons piled in heaps, which   4355
The French have seized from all parts of the region;
No man alive has ever seen their equal;
The duke sees them and sighs with sorrow deeply:
"By God in Paradise, the true Redeemer,
I do not think I've ever seen such people!   4360
Ah Charles, my lord, fine King and mighty leader,
How wrongfully you have come to besiege me!
May God and St. Maurice not let you leave here
Until you too have had your share of grieving —
If I live long enough, you shall receive it!"   4365
He cries aloud so all his men may hear him:
"Turn back with me, you brave knights of good breeding,
To Vienne town of high renown and regal!"
"My lord," they say, "your words shall be well heeded!"
They turn the reins of their war-steeds to leave there,   4370
And all the French rush forward to impede them
Astride their steeds of war well-armed and eager;
In the great press, back where the fight is fiercest,
Bides Oliver, who is both brave and fearless;
Without Lord God, Who died for all believers,   4375
He will have need of friends before the evening!
Now from the French a messenger goes speeding
To tell King Charlemagne, the proud of feature,
That Girart's men have come in force and fiercely
     To fight them at their tents.   4380

120

Before the King the messenger arrives
And cries aloud: "Fine lord, now you shall find
Who has the heart to help you in a fight!
Girart the duke, I'll not withhold or hide,

Has charged us in our tents the other side." 4385
The King hears this and both his cheeks turn white;
He calls Girbert of Tarragone aside,
Who comes to him not wasting any time,
And Roland, fully armed, moves up likewise;
On seeing him the King straightway inquires: 4390
"Tell me, fine nephew, by God Who gave us life,
Is our host armed, tell me without a lie?"
"Indeed we are, and we are many, Sire;
Sound out your horns so all may heed the sign!"
And so they do, to the tents on all sides; 4395
The King himself puts on his armor bright
And mounts his horse not wasting any time;
He grasps a pike whose blade is of sharp iron
And spurs his steed which leaps into its stride;
He rides ahead before all of his knights, 4400
Outrunning them more than an arrow's flight;
Girart asks Oliver, who's by his side:
"Tell me, fine nephew, do you not recognize
This rapid steed and he who sits astride?"
"I do not, lord, by God Who gave me life; 4405
But curse the cur who turns from him in fright!
Let us advance and see how he replies!"
Girart reponds: "We'll do as you desire!"
The duke turns round and spurs in a straight line
Towards the King, not wasting any time; 4410
He knows him not, and that is why he rides
    At Charlemagne the worthy.

121

Beneath Vienne the ranks swell on the plain;
With all his zeal Duke Girart spurs away
To joust against the strong King Charlemagne; 4415
Upon his shield he lands a blow so great
That to the top he splits the boards in twain;
The hauberk's strong and Charles himself is safe;
The splinters fly as the spear strikes and breaks;
Then Charles strikes him with all his rage and hate, 4420
Slashing the saddle behind Girart away

So that the duke is flung backwards and laid
Upon the croup of his good Gascon bay;
Girart feels this and his heart is afraid;
Like a brave knight he strains to sit up straight,   4425
Plying the stirrups with all the strength he may;
Then he draws forth his golden-hilted blade
And smites the rounded helm of Charlemagne;
Without Lord God and His most blessèd name,
And the strong coif of his bright coat of mail,   4430
Emperor Charles would surely have been slain:
"God," says the King, "Who Lazarus did raise,
It has been twenty years or more, I'd say,
Since royal France was mine as King to claim;
Since then I've met no prince so high in fame   4435
Who ever struck my helm with so much rage,
Unless the blow was from some Pagan knave!
But now this lord has struck me with such weight
That to my crown my head's all in a daze!
God, let me live to see him well repaid —   4440
Which he will be, if God gives me His aid!"
When Girart hears this speech and it is plain
That he has struck the noble Charlemagne,
He leaps straight off his Aragon destrier
And comes to Charles without one moment's waste,   4445
Kissing his foot and stirrup straightaway;
He begs pardon, for God and His name's sake,
From Charlemagne for striking by mistake;
Charles hears him cry, but no reply he makes;
Girart sees this and fills with great dismay,   4450
And sees the French approaching him in haste,
The Emperor's great host in full array —
So he remounts his Aragon destrier
And spurs it forth to run as fast it may
    Straight back to Vienne city.   4455

122

Beneath the rich and strong town of Vienne
A very fine and wide meadow extends;
An ancient wood is planted at one end

And there it is that both forces have met —
The men of Charles, so white of beard and head,   4460
And all of valiant-visaged Duke Girart's men:
"Mountjoy the fierce!" cry out aloud the French,
While Girart's men shout: "St. Maurice the blest!"
Behold, my lords, so many spears erect
With flags of Almerian silk bedecked!   4465
How well they strike! Not one stints of his strength!
How many horses there are riderless!
How many shields are shorn apart and cleft,
How many coats are ripped aside and rent!
Lone horses roam throughout the meadow's length —   4470
No one takes them, no one takes note of them;
Girart cries out in a loud voice and says:
"What are you at, my valiant-hearted men,
Whose wont it is to vie for knighthood's best?
Strike well and hard — do not spare one of them!"   4475
When this is said, his men take heart again;
Behold them break so many lances then
And leave French steeds of riders all bereft!
The man who falls has little lifetime left,
For he is crushed most awfully to death;   4480
Still Girart's men are in great need of help:
By force of arms they fall back from the press,
For the King's might is too great to contest;
The battle's tide turns against Girart's men,
        And their losses are heavy.   4485

123

Behold, my lords, a youth called Nevelon,
Girart's nephew, one of the best he's got;
He lifts his lance and shows the gonfalon;
Upon his shield he strikes one Eslion,
A counsellor of Charles the Emperor;   4490
He smites and splits the shield beneath the boss;
Eslion's safe, his coat of mail is strong,
But Nevelon strikes well and down he drops;
He draws his sword, whose hilt is gold-embossed,
And strikes once more on his round helmet's top;   4495

Down on the sand he sends the Frank headlong:
"Vienne!" he cries, "Barons and knights, strike on!"
He sees Girart and lifts his voice aloft:
"Uncle Girart, how feeble is our wrath!
But I shall fight beside you from now on   4500
    Amidst the blows of battle."

124

Below Vienne, beside the leafy trees,
The fight is fierce, I tell you truthfully;
Hernaut the Poitevin — lords, can you see
As he attacks Count Oliver the fierce?   4505
And Oliver is ready, lords, and keen;
He brandishes his pike and spurs his steed
To land a mighty blow upon his shield;
From edge to edge the boards are cleft and pierced;
The hauberk's strong, none of the mail is breached;   4510
Hernaut is saved from death or injury,
Though he is felled by the force of the spear;
Count Oliver draws rein and turns to leave:
"Vienne!" he cries and calls likewise: "Geneve!"
He sees Girart and meets him, drawing near;   4515
In a fierce voice, on meeting him he speaks:
"Uncle Girart, by God in truth tell me,
How did you fare in fighting that proud Peer
Whom we observed before as he raced here?"
Girart replies: "I fared most evilly!   4520
I am heart-sick at having struck my liege;
He will show me no mercy now or peace!"
But Oliver responds, his anger deep:
"Fine lord, we cannot turn round now and leave!
By God in truth, let us ride through the field   4525
And strike the French once more with all our zeal!"
Girart replies: "Nephew, most willingly!"
When this is said, they turn about their steeds:
My lords, behold the bitter strife proceed!
Behold so many shields split front to rear!   4530
The man who falls to ground there from his steed
Stands up no more, if no good friend is near;

The Vienne knights are forced back, piece by piece:
They can no more abide the might convened
On Charles's side, I tell you truthfully;   4535
Girart the duke, of courage high and fierce,
And Lord Hernaut and his son Aymeri
Regroup their force upon a hillock's peak;
Their boldest knights spur once more through the field
And strike great blows which those behind repeat;   4540
Through Charles's ranks they forge and force a breach;
The King sees this and groans in disbelief;
    His grief and rage are heavy.

125

The clash is great and dreadful is the fray;
The King calls forth Elinant and Gautier: 4545
"My lords," he says, "pay heed to what I say:
Select at once and lead off straightaway
Four hundred men of courage fierce and great;
Turn round your steeds and head them with all haste
Towards Vienne and beat them to their gates!   4550
This way none of these traitors shall escape!"
Roland cries out: "A wondrous plan, in faith!
Are not these rogues before us face to face?
Why should we seek them in some other place?
Since they are here, may God confound the knave   4555
Who would ride forth to find them once again!
Let us strike now, together in our rage,
And stop the mouths of their most bold this day!"
When this is said, Count Roland spurs away
Into the press, swinging Durendal's blade;   4560
Hot on his heels the French all do the same,
And more than seven thousand attack this way;
They hit the Vienne host and their ranks break;
If Girart stays, the loss will be too great
Of the best knights and bravest of his race: 4565
So he sounds out a horn without delay
To rally all his men across the plain;
Then he holds Oliver by his steed's rein,
To stop him tarrying in the fierce fray;

They leave the fight with all the haste they may,   4570
To reach Vienne, their city strong and brave:
Hot on their heels spur all their worthy race,
   Who close the gates behind them.

126

Girart's men reach Vienne and ride straight in;
They close the gates and raise the castle bridge;   4575
King Charles looks on and almost leaves his wits;
He calls aloud in his fierce pride and will:
"My worthy knights, assault these walls forthwith!
Who fails me now shall lose what's mine to give:
No town or tower of his in France exists,   4580
No march or city or fortress strongly-built,
That shall not fall, if he fails me in this!"
When this is said, they surge forth and begin:
The squires first run to the walls and hit
The solid stones with hammers and sharp picks;   4585
The Vienne knights stand at the top and tip
Upon their heads sharp stones and wood and sticks;
More than three score are struck by them and killed;
More than five score young squires of the French King
Drop from the walls and fall into the ditch: 4590
"True Emperor," says the bearded Naimes:
"Do you think you can take Vienne like this,
With its strong walls and its high battlements
And sturdy towers which long ago were built
By Pagan hands with all their power and skill?   4595
You will not take them as long as you shall live!
Send back to France and have your envoys bring
French engineers to help you conquer it:
When they arrive, then they can start to build
Machines of war to their design, wherewith   4600
These walls may be cast down to their last inch!"
The King hears this and blanches to his lips:
   He is so heavy-hearted.

127

These words are said by Naimes the white-bearded:
"True Emperor, I shall not hide my feelings; 4605
So help me God, your mind has lost its reason
If you think this fine town can be defeated
By storming it with climbing and with leaping!
The walls are high and have been raised by heathens;
By my faith in the blessèd Maid, believe me, 4610
You will not take them thus in seven years here!
Send back to France for the help that is needed
From engineers who know how to besiege it;
They will bring down these ancient walls and breach them."
When Charles hears this, he falls to heavy grieving, 4615
Then cries aloud once more: "Mountjoy, the fearsome!
What are you at, my fine and hardy liegemen?"
Then their assault begins once more, and fiercely
The Vienne force hurls sticks and stones to meet it;
See then fair Aude, the lovely, slender creature, 4620
Dressed in a silk woven in Almeria
With golden thread of perfect stitch and seaming;
Her eyes are green and rosy are her features
Atop the walls of the old town appearing;
When she beholds the fierce assault proceeding, 4625
She stoops to ground and lifts a stone, then heaves it
To strike a Gascon on his helm of Pavia:
All of its outer rim she breaks to pieces
And takes the Gascon's life — or very nearly!
Roland the valiant-visaged laughs to see it; 4630
The well-bred count calls out so she may hear him:
"We shall not take this town or ever seize it
At this one point, so help me blessèd Jesus,
For I shall not attack ladies, believe me!
But I shall not forsake this rampart either 4635
Without asking you for your name, fair creature!
Take no offense, fair maid, if I intreat you;
I do not ask with any evil meaning."
"My lord," she says, "then I shall not conceal it;
I am called Aude by the race which has reared me, 4640
And am the daughter of Renier of Geneva;
I am Oliver's sister, the fierce of feature,

And Girart's niece, who scorns a coward's weakness;
And my own blood is of the highest breeding;
I've never had a husband or a liege-lord,   4645
Nor shall I have, so help me blessèd Jesus,
If Lord Girart does not sanction or seek one,
And Oliver, who is bravery's beacon!"
Roland replies so that she does not hear him:
"By God the Son of Mary, how much it grieves me   4650
That I do not have you in my safe-keeping!
Without God's help I never shall achieve it,
For I must win the battle I've agreed to
    With her own Oliver!"

128

Fair Aude, the maiden wise of heart, remarks: 4655
"Sir knight, my lord, I have not for my part
Failed to reply in truth to all you've asked;
Now, if you please, tell me on your behalf
Where you were born and who your kinsmen are;
How well you bear that shield upon your arm,   4660
And that fine sword upon your hip held fast,
And that fine spear with its gonfalon clasped!
How you bestride that steed which in the charge
Runs with the speed of a loosed crossbow's shaft!
How you have hurt today this force of ours!   4665
You seem more fierce than all the force of France!
My thoughts tell me and I know in my heart
That your true love has all of beauty's charms!"
Roland hears this and answers with a laugh:
"Lady," he says, "you speak the truth, I grant!   4670
Be sure, there's none so fair as her as far
As here to Rheims or here to Rome, fair Aude,
    Nor elsewhere that I know of!"

129

When Roland hears the maid speak in this measure,
He does not speak all of his thoughts directly,   4675

But nonetheless his manner is most friendly:
"Young lady fair, without a lie I tell you
That I'm called Roland by all my friends and fellows."
When Aude hears this, then she is filled with pleasure:
"Are you that same whose name I have heard mentioned,   4680
He who has pledged to test my brother's mettle?
You little know of his valor and temper,
If you have sworn to meet in joust against him!
I swear to you in faith, I do regret it,
For you are thought to be my friend by many,   4685
As I have heard and have had many tell me!
Now by the faith you have pledged to the Emperor,
If you had caught me yesterday and held me,
Would you have felt enough pity to let me
Return unharmed from the heart of my enemy?"   4690
Roland hears this and all his senses tremble;
The count replies: "Young lady fair and tender,
Do not mock me, for sake of love I beg you."
The King calls to his side the count of Berry:
"My lord Lanbert, do not lie or dissemble: 4695
Who is that maid upon those ancient crenels
Who speaks with Roland and whom he too addresses?"
The count replies: "Upon my word, I tell you
That is young Aude of feature fair and splendid,
The daughter of Geneva's brave Lord Renier: 4700
The Lombard Enseis has sworn to wed her!"
King Charlemagne responds: "He'll never get her!
Roland has pledged his love to her directly!
One hundred men in full armor shall perish
Ere Enseis shall take her one step henceforth!"   4705
As this is said, see Roland turn, farewelling
The lovely maid, who leaves the walls directly;
The King looks on and teases Roland gently;
He says: "What vow have you made there, fine nephew,
To that fair maid with whom I have beheld you?   4710
If she has said or done something to vex you,
Please pardon her, for sake of love, I beg you."
Roland hears this and all his senses tremble;
     He bows his head with shame.

130

"Fine nephew Roland," says Charles in wisdom then: 4715
"Whoever gains the maid with whom at length
You have just spoken, I have gained naught myself!
For Oliver has ridden from Vienne
Together with one hundred knights and men
And stormed our ranks along one side of them: 4720
They have hewn off twenty of our men's heads
And taken prisoner scores of the rest;
The maiden Aude knew of this very well
And made of you the butt of joke and jest!"
Roland hears this and almost loses sense;   4725
With utmost rage his chin and cheek turn red;
When Charles beholds his nephew's great distress,
He comforts him with a fine tenderness;
He says: "Fine nephew, do not rage or lament!
For the maid's sake whom your heart has addressed,   4730
We shall return to our lodges and tents;
For sake of her our fighting we'll suspend!"
Roland replies: "My lord, as you think best."
They sound a horn and turn their horses' heads;
The Emperor returns to his own tent;   4735
Throughout the host the French disarm themselves
And very willingly that night they rest:
They eat their fill and drink to their content,
Then go to sleep as soon as daylight ends;
King Charlemagne of valiant prowess   4740
Sleeps in his tent, his body worn and spent,
For he has fought all day with all his strength:
The royal King sleeps deeply on his bed
And dreams a dream which fills with mighty dread
    The Emperor of France.   4745

131

Our Emperor is in his tent asleep;
The noble King, worn out and tired indeed
From bearing arms and fighting in the field,
Now dreams a dream that is dreadful and fierce:
He sees himself spur forth to take his ease   4750

Beside a river upon a mighty steed,
With a goshawk which he holds very dear;
One hundred squires ride with him blithe and free;
Then from Vienne he sees a falcon leave
For the great isle — it flies there at great speed;   4755
When it arrives, it rests upon a peak;
Three times it cries and makes so loud a screech
That Charlemagne and all the young knights hear;
If he could catch this bird, fierce Charles agrees,
Montpellier's gold would not buy its release: 4760
    He would take such joy in it.

132

Deep in his sleep the mighty King dreams more:
Now it appears to our great Emperor
That on his wrist he holds his flying hawk;
He lets it rise upon that falcon's course   4765
Which he had seen depart from Vienne's wall;
Upon the isle whose grass is green and tall
Both hunting-birds are standing claw to claw!
Then with great rage the two of them lunge forth
And strike each other in a fearsome assault   4770
Till both of them have lost much blood and force;
With their great wings they beat each other raw;
King Charlemagne looks on, fearful and fraught,
Lest he should lose the hawk which he adores;
As he looks on he turns his mind and thoughts   4775
In fervent prayer to the Almighty Lord,
Beseeching Him to save his flying-hawk;
So fervently the mighty King implores
That both those birds resolve on an accord
And mutual peace and show such love and joy   4780
They seem to kiss in fond embrace and warm;
The King sees this and he starts to rejoice
So fervently that he awakes with joy;
His body starts and he stands up distraught
To his soul's depths that he should dream it all;   4785
With his right hand he signs the Cross and calls
Upon Almighty God, Father and Lord,

To turn this dream to a good end and cause;
He summons then a very wise man forth
And tells him everything, omitting naught   4790
Of how, in his deep sleep, he dreamt and saw
Two noble birds which in fierce contest fought
And then made peace in friendship sweetly sworn;
When he hears this, the wise man shows great joy
And then says this: "O mighty Emperor,   4795
Be in no doubt about this dream of yours!
For I do think without one moment's pause
I can tell you the meaning it purports!
The fighting-bird, of this you may be sure,
Which flew down to the isle from Vienne's wall,   4800
Is Oliver the valiant-hearted lord,
Who will, I think, ride very shortly forth
From Vienne's gates, well-armed on his swift horse;
To keep the joust with Roland, as he swore,
He will fly like a falcon towards that shore;   4805
And that young hawk, I swear to you, my lord,
Who grappled with this flying-falcon's claws,
This is Count Roland, that brave nephew of yours,
Who will combat with his sharp, cutting sword
Young Oliver the valiant warrior;   4810
And they shall wound each other sick and sore
And then make peace, resolving an accord
Through God's own strength, Who is the Lord of all;
These two shall be fond comrades evermore,
      And you shall take joy in them!"   4815

133

The fierce-faced Emperor is glad indeed
To hear his dream explained so favorably;
He has no wish that night for further sleep
But to be dressed and shod immediately;
The night departs and light of day appears   4820
As the sun rises and shines brightly and clear;
The birds sing out below on Vienne's fields;
Inside the town Count Oliver appears
And he attends the church of St. Maurice

To hear God's word and blessing from the priest;   4825
Then he returns to the high hall, where he
Calls to his squire Garin to serve his needs:
"My friend," he says, "make haste and bring to me
My noblest clothes and finest fighting gear,
So I may dress without delay and leave."   4830
The squire replies: "Fine lord, most willingly!"
And goes to bring the count all that he needs;
The noble youth takes off immediately
His fair tunic and cloak of ermine dear,
So that he stands just in the shirt beneath;   4835
Then he puts on a fine doublet which gleams
With cloth of gold; he fears no arrow's steel
Or any weapon's piercing of its weave!
He moves to put his hauberk on, when see
The lord Girart arrive in company   4840
With Elinant and Gautier his peer!
Out of his hands he wrests the hauberk free
And in a courteous way begins to speak:
"For Lord God's sake, Oliver, nephew dear,
Forgo this fight to which you have agreed   4845
With Duke Roland, a valiant knight indeed
And noble vassal with weapons in the field!
A master carpenter cutting his beams
To make a room or dwelling does not wield
His axe aloft so skillfully as he!   4850
For all Gaifier's gold I would not see
Him joust with you and cause you injury;
My happy heart could never more be cheered."
"Though all Bavaria were offered me,
And all the land to Poitiers town from here,   4855
I'd not put off this fight, whoever pleads;
Now I must arm myself with every speed;
     For far too long I tarry."

134

"Dear nephew Oliver," brave Girart says:
"For Lord God's sake, Who suffered mortal pain   4860
Upon the Holy Cross to save His race,
Forgo this fight, fine boy, I urge again!

Roland the duke is fearsome in his rage;
There is no knight his equal in the fray."
Says Oliver: "Lord, I am not afraid!   4865
No fear of losing limb, nor offer made
Of gaining wealth shall cause me to refrain
From riding forth to fight Roland this day;
I've pledged to go and will not stop or stay;
I trust in God to guard me as He may;   4870
No blow can harm the man His arm keeps safe!
Uncle Girart, let me prepare now, pray!
You have caused me, I think, too much delay;
    It is high time I left here."

135

Just as the count is arming for the fight,   4875
Behold a Jew called Joachim arrive!
On cheek and chin his beard is lily-white;
Lords, when Pilate was captured for his crime
Of letting Jesus Christ be crucified —
Although I think revenge was wrought in time   4880
By Emperor Vespasian the wise,
Who rounded up, or so the history writes,
All of the Jews whom he could find alive
In Salem town the praiseworthy and prized
And marched them through the gates and took their lives —   4885
Since that same hour which I have just described,
This Jew has lived in Vienne with his tribe;
He's a rich man, of wealth and fortune high,
Who gives so much to barons of the shire
That they're prepared to let him live and thrive;   4890
Now he beholds the youth and speaks his mind:
"Oliver, brother," the ancient graybeard cries:
"Take these small gifts from me into your fight!
King Charles of St. Denis has none so fine."
The count hears this and sees them and admires;   4895
He clasps the Jew around his shoulders tight
And would have kissed him, had he believed in Christ!
The noble count most courteously replies:
"Give me these gifts, Joachim, friend of mine;

And if God grants, the King of Paradise,   4900
That I return from this joust with my life,
Then your own son shall straightway be baptised
And be dubbed knight ere seven days expire;
I'll give him arms and a fine horse to ride
And a large part of my own lands likewise."   4905
"May God forbid," this Joachim replies:
"That my own son should ever be baptised!
By God's own voice I swear I'd rather die
And see my son cast in the blazing fire!"
When Oliver hears this he laughs outright,   4910
As do the counts and marquises and knights;
The worthy Jew picks up the gifts meanwhile
    And brings them to Count Oliver.

136

This Joachim does not delay or stop;
He gives the gifts to valiant Oliver,   4915
Displaying them upon a table-top;
An Archbishop blesses them one by one,
In Lord God's name signing them with the Cross,
For the Jew's sake, of hoary beard and locks,
Who has held them within his house so long;   4920
Then the Jew says: "Let him be armed hereon,
For you can see that this is what he wants;
In these fine shoes let him be swiftly shod —
There's been no better made since Solomon!
Then fit these spurs of peerless value on: 4925
I bought them from a pagan Slav far-off,
One hundred pounds in gold mangons their cost;
With clusters of rich gems they are embossed,
Which are worth more than the town of Mâcon,
So I have heard and do not think it wrong."   4930
Girart replies: "With the blessing of God!"
The duke takes them without one moment's loss
And clips them to the young man's heels, which on
His ermine cloak he steadies as he does;
Like a brave knight he counsels Oliver —   4935
    For he is of his family.

137

They dress him in a coat of Eastern mail
Both strong and light, the lightest ever made:
A serving-man could carry twelve the same;
No arm on earth, no dart or cutting blade   4940
Could damage in the least this hauberk's chains,
They are so strong — no better could he crave;
King Aeneas won it from Eliné
In the great war before Troy on the plain
Where Paris, son of King Priam, was slain,   4945
And his brother Hector fell to his fate;
They all were killed, defeated or enslaved,
And their tall towers cast to the ground and razed;
There was no tower or high wall that remained:
Each brick of them lay broken on the plain;   4950
No mortal man escaped the battle, save
King Aeneas, for whom God's love was great;
He fled with his own father, making escape
Upon a barge across the ocean's waves;
Aboard he cured with skill his wounds and pain;   4955
Aeneas wore this coat of Eastern mail
But lost it near Maradant in a fray
Fought in a forest with Roboant, they say;
A powerful knight slew Aeneas that day,
A soldier from the ranks of France the brave,   4960
And he won then this coat of Eastern mail;
When he returned, straight to Vienne he came
Where Joachim paid him much in exchange;
In the Jew's treasure-chests since then it's lain;
He's given it to Oliver this day,   4965
The well-bred count, the offspring bold and brave
    Of Renier of Geneva.

138

The count girds on a sword with a sharp edge;
The blade is strong but too hard in its strength: 4970
It broke in half too soon below Vienne
And Aude the maid filled with dismay and dread
And for her brother's sake was in distress —

As you, if you so please, shall hear yourselves,
If my song is well heeded and well said!
A rounded shield he hangs about his neck,   4975
Painted in gold and brightest blue, whose crest
Depicts a fish deep in the ocean's depths;
The shield's as hard as any anvil's head;
This Joachim of hoary beard and head
Obtained it from a pagan in Valsore,   4980
Who was well paid for what he had to sell:
He gained a goblet full of deniers!
Girart the duke, without delay or let,
Calls on his squires to seek out and to fetch
A good war-horse with a gold saddle set   4985
For Oliver, who mounts with no regrets;
Lords, many a tear by lovely Aude is shed,
And Duke Girart consoles her much and well:
"Nephew," the valiant-visaged duke says then:
"May God, Who makes the sky and dew, direct   4990
The victory to you in this day's quest!
      And safeguard you from slaughter!"

139

"My nephew dear," proclaims Girart the bold:
"To Lord our God, Who suffered mortal woe
Upon the Cross to save all Christian folk,   4995
I do commend this day your life and soul!
You do not go to gain wealth of your own
But to defend your uncle from reproach;
Take this good horn, fine nephew, as you go,
And drape it on your shield around your throat;   5000
When you ride down Vienne and reach below,
Sound it on high as you face the French host,
So Charles may hear and all his knights may know
That you have come to fight for me alone."
"My lord," says Oliver, "it shall be so."   5005
He takes the horn and fears none as he goes,
Except Lord God on His majestic throne,
And Lord Roland, so fierce and feared a foe —
Though in the field he felled him when he drove

An awesome thrust right through his horse's bones!   5010
The worthy count struck many a valiant blow:
May Jesus Christ have mercy on his soul!
Now when the count mounts on his horse he shows
His banded shield against his bosom close,
While in his fist a cutting spear he holds,   5015
Which flies a flag fixed with five nails of gold;
Count Renier of Geneva, the wise and bold,
Frets for his son and weeps gently and low,
As does the brave lord of Biaulande, Hernaut,
And Aymeri the valiant knight also;   5020
The maiden Aude commends him to God's hold
And Oliver delays no more but goes
Out of the gate on his appointed road;
Beneath Vienne he rides down to the Rhône,
Where he embarks and crosses on a boat;   5025
Upon the bank he mounts again and goes
At rapid pace across the field and slope;
He takes the horn and gives it three long blows
With such a force and with such fearsome notes
That in their tents the French all hear below;   5030
They see him come, three thousand knights all told:
"Count Oliver's bewitched!" they cry, "Behold
How every inch of his fine armor glows!
If Roland seeks a fight, then one is close,
And fiercer far than any yet he's known!"   5035
An envoy turns and with all speed he goes
To tell Roland of Oliver's approach:
"He's armed and mounted and on the isle alone,
For he is keen to keep the pledge he spoke
In Charles's tent, when he gave you his oath."   5040
Roland hears this and a great joy he shows;
He says: "May You be praised, Lord God of Hosts!
You have brought me what I desired the most!"
He calls straightway for weapons and for clothes,
And those in charge without delay bring both;   5045
The count is clad in the fine arms he owns:
He straps his jeweled helm and his mail-coat
And girds his sword whose hilt is burnished gold,
And which is called Durendal, as you know;

He won it from Aumon, a Pagan rogue;   5050
The Emperor calls to him in these tones:
"My nephew dear, hear me and be not loth!
For Lord God's sake, Who bore the Cross's woe,
Forgo this fight! I urge you not to go!
And Oliver the wise will then, I hope,   5055
Ride back inside Vienne among his folk;
For I would not for two cities of gold
See him lose limb or life's blood from your blows,
Nor see yourself struck down by some ill stroke!"
"You urge in vain," says Roland, "for I won't   5060
Hold back my hand for all the wealth you own!
For I have pledged my word, as you well know,
And will not be forsworn or break my troth;
There's nothing any man can do or hope
That will prevent me riding at my foe!   5065
If I should break my promise and my oath,
    My shame would be most heavy."

140

"Fine nephew dear," says fierce-faced Charlemagne:
"Since you desire it so and it is plain
That you will fight whatever I might say,   5070
I do commend your life to Lord God's grace,
That He may guard and keep your body safe
And spare Lord Oliver from grief or grave."
"Uncle most sweet," replies Roland the brave:
"For Lord God's sake, Who on the Cross was nailed,   5075
Let none alive ride after me this day;
For all the gold in Paris I'd not be blamed
For wronging Oliver in any way."
"None shall," says Charlemagne, "I pledge my faith."
Roland replies: "Much thanks, in Lord God's name."   5080
This said, they bring his Arab steed straightway
And Roland mounts without the stirrup's aid;
Around his neck a curving shield they drape
And in his hand a burnished spear they lay,
Which flies a flag fixed with five golden nails;   5085
Through all the tents he rides without delay,

Comes to the Rhône and does not hesitate
But rides across on his fine destrier;
Straight for the isle the courtly warrior makes,
Where Oliver the valiant-hearted waits;   5090
The powerful duke spurs forth at a fast pace
And Oliver rides forward in great haste,
His heavy shield held up before his face
    With all his strength and temper.

141

When Oliver sees Roland's fierce intention,   5095
He rides at him with all his strength and temper;
Duke Roland rides till they are close together
And then he cries: "Knight, say your name and tell me:
Are you Bavarian, German or Frenchman,
From Normandy, from Flanders or from Berry?"   5100
Count Oliver responds and says: "God help me,
Roland, do you not know me or remember?
I am the son of the most worthy Renier,
Geneva's lord of such prowess and merit;
My uncle is Girart the fierce of mettle,   5105
And my cousin, I am not loth to tell you,
Is Aymeri of fierce and fiery temper,
From whom the other day you stole a destrier!
I have come here in some part to avenge him;
The other day I do remember well too   5110
That you seized Aude my sister fair, intending
To bear her forth on your horse to your tent there!
Thanks be to God, our true Father in Heaven,
My burnished sword of steel came to her rescue;
And how your spurs helped you, I'll not forget it,   5115
When you rode back to Charles's host and fled me!
I say this not to blame you or offend you,
Rather, most noble knight, I do request you
To make our peace with your uncle's displeasure;
You shall have Aude, my sister, and shall wed her."   5120
Roland replies: "Your plea to me is senseless;
I shall lead you beside my horse well tethered
Right back to France and to a prison cell there;

I shall have Aude, whoever may regret it!"
Count Oliver responds: "You shall not ever,   5125
    As long as I'm alive!"

142

Count Oliver is full of valiant zeal,
At every point opposing Roland's speech,
Addressing him in truth most angrily:
"By God the Son of Mary, I repeat   5130
What I have said: it is madness indeed
For you to think in your great knavery
That you will make my uncle bend the knee!
He will not bow to you while he still breathes,
Nor be your slave for all of Normandy!"   5135
Roland replies: "Your plea's senseless to me;
I do not care for your words in the least;
If God preserves Durendal's burnished steel,
I'll have your head before compline is here!"
Says Oliver: "You shall not, I believe!   5140
Girart the duke, my valiant-visaged liege,
    Would be too much the loser!"

143

Both worthy warriors are on the isle;
There never were two knights so fierce and fine;
King Charles's nephew addresses Renier's child: 5145
"Vassal, let us leave all your pleas aside!
I have come here to conquer Vienne's pride,
This strong-walled town whose ramparts are so high,
For Charlemagne, who is my liege by right;
If you show honor, he'll honor you likewise."   5150
Count Oliver, the well-bred youth, replies
With words for which he should be praised and prized
And cherished by all men of noble line:
"Ah Roland, lord, noble and well-bred knight!
For Lord God's sake, Who suffered mortal spite   5155
Upon the Cross to save all Christian lives,
I urge you to make peace between both sides;

You shall have Aude to be your wedded wife
And all Vienne to govern and to guide;
I shall convince Duke Girart to comply;   5160
And from now on in fearsome frays and fights
I shall be your flag-bearer close by your side."
Roland replies: "Your sermoning's ill-timed!
When I've slain you with my steel blade, then I
Shall have Vienne and lovely Aude besides,   5165
    In spite of all your kinsmen!"

144

Says Oliver of bold and valiant heart:
"My lord Roland, for love of God hold hard!
What you have said can never come to pass;
Instead, do what for love of you I've asked: 5170
For love of God, Who never fails the task,
Make peace and let us be comrades in arms!
For all Ponthieu I would not see you harmed
Or taken prisoner — for at the last
I know full well that there is every chance   5175
That all my friends would bear the blame of France,
And then the King and my uncle Girart
Would nevermore be friends by choice or chance;
Instead, do what I urge you to and ask,
Then I and my own uncle of valiant heart,   5180
Will be your men and swear it with hands clasped."
"In truth," says Roland, "you'll not slip from my grasp!
For I shall slay you here or hold you fast
And hand you to the King who raised me — Charles!
And he shall lead you to his jail in France,   5185
Where you shall lie, though I lie not, I grant,
Till you are banned from your own land and ours;
Then I shall rule Vienne and have fair Aude,
And your uncle, who has betrayed King Charles,
Shall flee in fear, a beggar and outcast."   5190
"Your speech is fantasy!" says Oliver:
"And I'd be mad to ask more than I've asked!
Good God, why did I seek peace at the start:
I was a fool and a foul recreant!

God help me now, for I am in Your charge!   5195
My lord Roland, since things are as they are,
And I can find no mercy in your heart,
Do not say hence I failed my plighted task;
I do defy you now, so be on guard!
I've warned you well, so let the contest start!"   5200
Roland replies: "I've heard you to the last!"
If you could see how stubbornly they part!
Each spurs his Arab steed upon a path
Which parts the pair one furlong and a half;
As they turn round each lifts aloft his lance   5205
And clasps his sturdy shield to his left arm;
Then they ride hard across the flowering grass,
 The one against the other.

145

If you could see how stubbornly they face,
Seizing their spears and flourishing their blades,   5210
Digging their spurs into their destriers,
Then you would say that they were the best pair
In all the world to justify their claims!
Upon each quartered shield great blows they lay
Beneath the boss which break the boards away   5215
And cause each mighty lance to split and break;
Their coats are strong, they cannot pierce the mail;
The noble knights collide with such a weight
That both their steeds collapse beneath the strain;
Down to their knees they fall, then rise again   5220
As both men pass each other and ride away;
Then they turn back like falcons after prey,
 The one against the other.

146

Count Roland sits astride his Gascon stallion;
He draws his blade Durendal from its scabbard   5225
And lands a blow high on the helmet-panels
Which knocks to ground the garland jewels they carry;
The blow drives on and in its downward passage

It strikes Oliver's steed behind the saddle;
It parts the felt of the vermilion padding   5230
And splits the Gascon steed along its backbone;
Deep down beside the horse's bowels it travels,
Smiting the spur of gold, slicing and slashing
The tip away beside Oliver's ankle;
Into two halves the blow bisects the Gascon   5235
And rushes on till in the ground it hammers;
Count Oliver the brave is left there standing!
Roland cries out: "Mountjoy for Charles the valiant!
This day Vienne shall be destroyed and captured,
Which false Girart has held in traitorous fashion!   5240
He will receive a bitter wage to thank him —
Like a vile rogue he'll hang upon the gallows!"
Says Oliver: "You are a foolish braggart!
Lord God, Who pardoned Longinus his action,
Decides on all: He may stretch forth His hand here   5245
In my support against you and your valor;
I have come here to face you in this battle
For the defense of Vienne and its palace;
You shall not gain one spur of it in value,
Unless you pay one hundred pounds in mangons!"   5250
He draws his sword, like a lion in anger,
Advancing then like a courageous vassal;
Girart the duke is filled with fear and anguish
There in the tower of his fortress and palace;
The wealth of Solomon would not distract him: 5255
For a long time he says nothing, but stands there;
When he does speak, he calls in fearsome fashion
On the most blessèd Lord and God of mankind:
"Glorious Father, Who suffered mortal Passion,
And lifted Lazarus from death's dark chasm,   5260
And pardoned all the sins of Mary Magdalen,
And saved Jonah from the great whale's entrapping:
As this is true and we believe it gladly,
Withhold this day the life of my own champion
From Roland's hands, the nephew of Charlemagne!   5265
    If not, my joy will perish!"

147

At a small window's ledge the fair Aude leans;
She cries and sighs, her hand upon her cheek,
When she beholds her brother cast afield,
Flung on his feet by his steed from Castile,   5270
Down from the saddle of his most worthy steed;
Within her breast the maiden feels such grief
That her heart nearly breaks in two beneath;
She runs off to a chapel wherein she kneels
Before the altar with this secret appeal: 5275
"Glorious God," the fair maiden entreats:
"Who in the Virgin's womb was bred to breathe,
Whom many sinners exhort in their great need,
Grant that such news of both counts comes to me
Which shall please both Girart and Charles's ear,   5280
   The Emperor of France."

148

Aude swoons upon the chiselled-marble stones;
Her fresh, long gown and her fine ermine cloak
Are damp with tears, for she has fretted so;
She begs Lord God in gentle, honest tones,   5285
Who came to earth to bring His people hope:
"Glorious Lord, let Your great mercy flow
On these two knights, for I do love them both;
Let them neither be maimed or slain as foes!"
We shall leave Aude, whose heart is wrung with woe,   5290
And tell once more of Roland, famed of old,
And Oliver whose heart was strong and bold,
Who now, on foot, must strike Roland a blow!
He lifts his sword, whose hilt is seamed with gold,
And deals Roland's striped helm so fierce a stroke   5295
That he smites off the garland-jewels it boasts;
The worthy blade drives on and as it goes
It strikes the steed before its saddle-bows
And splits the beast between its shoulder-bones;
Down to the field the blow falls unopposed   5300
And in a heap both horse and rider roll;
When he sees this, joy fills Oliver's soul:

If half of France were given him to own,
And Orléans and Rheims were his to hold,
I do not think he'd be as glad of those   5305
As of the count he has unhorsed and thrown
    Upon Vienne's large island!

149

If you had been beneath Vienne, my lords,
When Oliver and Roland faced and fought!
There never were two knights as brave before,   5310
So bold of heart and so well-skilled in war!
How well they struck each other with their great swords
And laid huge blows upon those bucklers' boards!
Out of their helms the precious gems were torn
And sparks flew off and lit the land abroad;   5315
No man alive in these days ever saw
A fight to match the combat I record;
And those who saw it then would nevermore
Behold a duel where such fierce blows were scored;
Girart the duke stands on his castle walls   5320
With Lord Hernaut, the ruler of Biaulande,
And Aymeri the noble, valiant boy;
Renier of Geneva laments, distraught
For Oliver the son whom he adores:
"Mary, blest Saint," he weeps aloud and calls: 5325
"Safeguard this day my brave son Oliver!
Let him not be defeated or overborne!"
And Charlemagne from his heart's depth implores:
"Mary, blest Saint, keep Roland in your ward!
    He shall be my successor!"   5330

150

Beneath Vienne upon the sandy isle
Both valiant knights are locked in mortal strife;
Like two fierce champions they strain and strive;
Each shows no mercy upon the other's life,
For both are fiercer than leopard is or lion;   5335
I do not know who should be praised the higher,

For both of them were of such fame and might
That neither one would flee from any fight
One spur in length, though Samson's wealth enticed!
With naked steel what lusty blows they strike!   5340
Their shields are split apart, their helmets spliced,
Whose rings of gold serve little use this time:
They slice through them like silk saddle-cloth ties!
The clash of steel flings forth a blaze of light
As all the sparks fly off on every side;   5345
Both of these knights are so intent and wild
That neither fears the other one a mite;
With such high rage and such rampaging strides
They stalk each other, it is a wondrous sight!
The lion-shields of both are broken wide   5350
And every ring upon their hauberks bright,
So that, beneath, their actons show inside;
Without the help of Lord God Jesus Christ
Neither of them shall leave this fight alive;
Up in Vienne, in the main tower on high,   5355
Lady Guibourc is filled with woe and spite,
As is the sweet, fair-visaged Aude alike;
They tear their hair with constant tears and sighs
And wring their hands and wail aloud and cry:
"Alas, Vienne! Better by far that fire   5360
Should burn your walls on each and every side
Until no tower or any room survived,
Than for your sake such knights should risk their lives!
For we know well, if one of them should die,
France will be ruined and all its realm likewise,   5365
And all this land destroyed amidst the strife."
Fair Aude the maid does not relent but finds
Hernaut her uncle, whose fame and name are high,
And speaks this way to worthy Biaulande's Sire:
"Tell us, fine uncle, and give us your advice,   5370
How with no blame or shame we may contrive
That these two knights may soon be reconciled!"
"I can do nothing," the worthy man replies:
"It is Girart and Charles the King who fight
With common fault and common hate and pride!   5375
Our old grandsire, we know this to be right,

Good Duke Beuvon of beard and whiskers white,
Gave not one ounce either in coin or kind
Of fealty to Charles in all his life,
    For Vienne and its honors."   5380

151

Upon the isle the valiant vassals face;
They are on foot, for their fast destriers
Have been hacked down by their cutting steel blades;
Roland speaks forth, whose heart was ever brave:
"Oliver, lord, by all my Christian faith,   5385
I never saw a man who had your grace;
We two oppose each other in this place
And shall strike blows in a fearsome affray
Till one of us is made to yield or slain;
No mortal man is here to lend us aid;   5390
And yet I swear, in God's majestic name,
I see two ladies in Vienne's hall ornate
Who cry aloud in anguish for our sakes
And make lament for Lord Oliver's fate;
So help me God, I pity their complaints!"   5395
"You speak the truth, indeed," Oliver says:
"They are Guibourc, whose heart is wise with age,
And Aude my sister, so fair of form and face;
These two are sad with sorrow for my sake;
But if Lord God, Who made the world, dictates   5400
That I return to them alive, I'll say
So much to Aude before tomorrow fades,
That if her wish to marry you must fail,
She'll wed no other lord all of her days,
    But seek a nun's life rather."   5405

152

Both noble knights are facing on the field,
Where they strike blows with all their strength and zeal;
Roland the duke, whose face with valor gleams,
Smites mighty blows with his great sword of steel,
Called Durendal, whose valor was well seen   5410

At Roncevaux on that black day and bleak
When it was cleft at last from Roland's keep;
And Oliver lifts his own blade and wields
A mighty blow at Roland's circled shield;
Right in the middle of the stout boss it beats,   5415
But drawing it, he finds it is stuck deep,
And by the hilt the blade snaps as it's freed;
Before Vienne the cry goes up in brief
That Oliver, whose face with valor gleams,
Has snapped his sword into a paltry piece;   5420
When Aude hears this, she swoons and falls with grief;
She moans aloud, when rising to her feet,
And calls St. Mary in a loud voice indeed:
"Oliver, brother, how hard your destiny!
If I lose you, God has forgotten me!   5425
I never shall be Roland's wife, it seems,
The best of men to gird a sword of steel!
A veiled nun, alas, is what I'll be!
Mary, most blest," fair Aude the wise entreats:
"I see my brother fighting in yonder field   5430
With my beloved, who spoke his love for me;
Whoever dies, I shall go mad with grief!
Set them apart, St. Mary, Heaven's Queen!"
Girart hears this and the blood leaves his cheeks;
He lifts her up and bids her with all speed   5435
Brought to a church with noble company;
They comfort her with great difficulty;
When news of all of this greets Charles's ear,
One thousand knights lament across the field;
The King himself, in private, weeps forth tears   5440
    Upon his furs of marten.

153

When Oliver beholds his sword-blade severed
Into two lengths which lie upon the meadow,
And when he sees his horse struck through the center
And sees his shield pierced through the boards and shredded,   5445
Then rest assured, my lords, his heart is heavy!
For he can see no arm at all to help him;

He looks around to all parts of the meadow
And sees himself hemmed in in each direction
With no means of escape from there whatever;   5450
He's so aggrieved he almost leaves his senses;
But then his heart displays its valiant temper:
He'd rather die with honor on this meadow
Than have it thought as cowardice by any
That he made show of fleeing from his death there;   5455
So he moves up with his fists at the ready:
Observed by all he is prepared to wrestle;
But Roland sees the noble lord's intention
And speaks like a well-tutored knight and tells him:
"Lord Oliver, how proud your great prowess is!   5460
For I can see that your steel sword has severed,
And I have one which is so fine and splendid
That it cannot be chipped or broken ever!
I am the King of the French kingdom's nephew —
If I should wound or vanquish you defenceless,   5465
Then all my life I'd bear the blame and blemish
That I had slain a man who held no weapon!
Lord, seek a sword freely and in no peril —
And a full cask of wine or claret's measure!
My thirst is great, I'm not ashamed to tell you!"   5470
When Oliver hears this, he thanks him gently:
"Roland, my lord, my thanks for this concession
Of your own honor, which honors my protection;
Now, if you please, for your own body's welfare
Take some repose a while upon this meadow   5475
Till I have spoken with the boatman who led me
Across the flow to this isle on his ferry."
Roland replies: "I shall do, with great pleasure."
And Oliver, of valiant mood and mettle,
Strides to the shore, waiting no more, intending   5480
     To hail the boatman there.

154

Count Oliver strides forth without delay
And calls upon the boatman in all haste:
"My friend, give ear to me!" the good count says:

"Go to Vienne as quickly as you may   5485
And tell Girart, my uncle bold and brave,
That by its silver hilt I've snapped my blade,
And he must send a second in its place,
So I may fight for all the rights he claims
In Lord God the Almighty Father's name,   5490
And St. Maurice, in whom I set my faith;
And bid him send a cask of wine the same,
For Charles's nephew Roland's thirst is great."
The boatman says: "My lord, I shall obey."
He boards his boat and setting off straightway   5495
He sails across and lands upon the plain;
Straight to Vienne he runs as fast he may,
For Oliver bids him to make all haste,
And he knows well how urgent is the aid;
He climbs up now into the hall of state   5500
Where he sees Lord Girart and loudly says:
"My lord, for God our great Redeemer's sake,
Brave Oliver through me asks you this day
To help him in his need amidst the fray:
Beneath its silver hilt he's snapped his blade   5505
And bids you send a second one straightway,
And a full cask of well-spiced wine the same:
For Charles's nephew Roland's thirst is great."
Girart replies: "As the Lord God dictates!
    Roland is very noble."   5510

155

Girart the duke does not delay at all,
But straightaway to the good boatman calls:
"My friend, may God defend you and your cause!
Speed with my help to noble Oliver!
So help me God, you'll earn a rich reward!   5515
Go, take these keys to my wine-cellar's door
And take tenfold the wine that you ask for
And bid the steward to bring the gold cup forth!
I'll have brought here to you two worthy swords:
One is my own, the other Renier wore,   5520
Geneva's lord and father of Oliver."

The boatman says: "I'll gladly do this all."
Now Joachim bides there upon the boards,
The worthy Jew of noble deeds and thoughts,
Who gave the arms to Oliver before;   5525
He hears the cries and sighs of many a voice
And the grim news of the boatman's report,
    And hastens to his dwelling.

156

When the Jew hears the cries and sighing made
And the grim news the boatman has made plain,   5530
That Oliver has snapped in two his blade,
Then he turns back to his own home in haste
To fetch a sword of great honor and fame:
For more than five score years he's kept it safe;
It was once Closamont's, whose fame was great   5535
As Emperor of mighty Rome the praised:
He lost the sword in woodland grass the day
Of that most fearsome fight, when he was slain
By the Pagan Malques of Valsegree;
He fell, his head clean severed by Malques,   5540
And from its sheath the good sword flew away;
The grass was thick where it was lost and lay;
Reapers, a long time after, chanced on the place:
One of their scythes was split by its sharp blade;
On seeing it they raised it up again   5545
And took it to the Pope in Rome straightway;
He saw how fine it was, with gold inlaid,
And the gold hilt with which it was ornate;
And in the words which he saw there engraved
He found it written, this is the truth I state,   5550
That Halteclere was this fine weapon's name,
And that in Rome it was crafted and made;
Manificans designed it and gave it shape,
An artisan of high repute and fame;
The Pope bade that it be well shone again   5555
And kept it in St. Peter's from that same day;
King Pépin took it forth, of France the famed,
When he first wore the crown which he had claimed;

In recompense Duke Beuvon gained the blade,
And he gave it to his Jew in exchange 5560
For many a pound of goods and gold in weight;
All since that time the Jew has kept it safe
And not one word was heard of it again
Till now, when Joachim gives it away
To Oliver, the son worthy of grace, 5565
   Of Renier of Geneva.

157

The worthy Jew, of noble heart and mind,
Brings forth straightway the burnished blade of iron
And gives it to Girart the warrior-knight;
He, in his turn, hands it to a good squire; 5570
A second sword he gives him ere he climbs
Upon his horse's back and starts to ride
Without delay down to the river-side;
The good boatman takes him across the tide
Where Marquis Oliver towards him strides; 5575
The squire tends him those two fine swords of iron;
The count selects the better one and tries
Fine Halteclere, and does not change his mind,
Handing the second one back to his squire;
Then he fills up the golden cup with wine 5580
And kneels before Sir Roland upon the isle;
He takes the cup — his need of it is high —
And slakes his thirst, drinking for a long time;
Count Roland drinks, and as he does, the squire
Sees that his neck is bent down to the wine, 5585
And thinks to help his lord in a low wise:
Out of its sheath he draws his sword of iron
With full intent to strike the noble knight
Across his neck, not sparing him one mite;
When Oliver beholds this and his eye 5590
Catches the glint of bare steel in the light,
He hastens up and rushing on the squire
He lifts his fist and with a mighty swipe
He fells the squire before him in a trice!
When this is done, he rails at him and cries: 5595

"Low wretch! I loved you well before this time;
At Pentecost I would have dubbed you knight!
Now you have lost any reward of mine!
Tomorrow morning, take to your heels and fly!
If I find you tomorrow, after I've dined,   5600
I'll have you hung or flung into the fire,
Or have you dragged by horses till you die
Like a foul thief, the noose around you tight!
You'll rue your wish to touch a worthy knight
    In such a wicked manner."   5605

158

When Roland's drunk enough to slake his need,
He calls Count Oliver, his anger keen:
"Let be your speech with that low wretch! If he
Had struck me down, all France would be aggrieved,
With all the realms on every side and reach;   5610
And the large bands of knights the Emperor keeps
Would be bereft this day of joy and zeal;
But let us speak no more of his deceit —
May he go to the devils, his brethren breed!
Sir, take your arms and go back to the field,   5615
For we have stayed too long at leisure here!
This day Girart the duke shall yet know fear,
This lord who holds Vienne traitorously;
When all is done, the payment he'll receive
Will be to hang for his great treachery!"   5620
Says Oliver: "That is a foolish speech!
All rests with God, the Lord of all and each,
Whose gentle hand will save him, if He please!
I trust in Him with all of my belief,
And in my arms and in my flashing steel   5625
To give me strength and the vigor and means
    To champion my uncle."

159

When Oliver hears plainly what is said
By Duke Roland, who answers him with threats,
He grips his shield and grasps it to his breast;   5630

If it were not unworthy to relent,
He'd not fight on for all Hungary's wealth;
He wields his sword, sharp, shining Halteclere,
And Roland lifts Durendal's burnished edge;
At Oliver he rushes then and sends   5635
A mighty blow at his Pavian helm;
All that it meets it splits apart and rends;
Down to the circle-base the sword deflects;
Without St. Mary's son, without God's help,
Down to his ears he would have split his head;   5640
But the blade slips and slides towards the left,
And on his floral shield the force descends;
The targe's not worth a clove of garlic then!
It's reft apart and cleft from end to end,
And the strong byrnie's skirts are cut to shreds;   5645
Down to the ground the great sword drives unchecked;
When Oliver feels this, he is incensed!
"God and my Lady, most blest Mary!" he says:
"Protect my limbs and guard my life from death!
By Roland's blows I know he's not in jest!   5650
I am unworthy, if I don't strike him next!"
He wields his sword, his trusted Halteclere,
And strikes Roland on his Pavian helm;
On its left side it's reft apart and cleft;
Down to the coif the great sword drives unchecked;   5655
But the Lord God guards Roland with His help:
Down to his ears he does not split his head —
The sword deflects and drives down with such strength
That the whole boss on the strong shield is cleft;
Down to the ground the burnished sword descends: 5660
"You spare me not at all!" Count Roland says;
When this blow's done, they move up once again
Towards each other with the fiercest intent;
Bracing their shields each one against their breast,
They swing their blades of steel with all their strength;   5665
So fierce a fight was never heard by men,
For both these knights were of such great prowess
That neither one would ever cede one step
Before the other, though losing life instead!
     So high and fierce their courage.   5670

160

Both of these knights are very fierce and brave;
Leopard nor lion have more courage than they;
The blows they strike no armor can sustain
And it's a marvel how long they fight and face;
The maiden Aude is very much afraid,   5675
Inside Vienne, high in the hall of state;
With a true heart she starts to pray and says:
"Glorious God, in Your most blessèd name,
Who made the earth, the seas, the fish and made
The firmament according to Your ways;   5680
Who made Adam out of the earth and clay,
And made his wife, who was called Eve, and gave
All Paradise for their enjoyment, save
An apple-tree, whose fruit, Lord, You forbade —
They ate of it and all their gain was pain,   5685
And still their heirs must bear the shame and blame;
Inside the Virgin's womb made Incarnate,
You came to earth born as a little Babe
In Bethlehem, we know this in our faith;
Inside the temple of Solomon You came,   5690
Held in the arms of Simeon the Saint;
And three kings journeyed from their mighty domains
In search of You and Your merciful Grace;
Throughout his realm Herod in wicked rage
Took all the Innocents and had them slain,   5695
Thinking that he would root You out this way;
For thirty years, we know, on earth You stayed
With Your Apostles, preaching Your Holy Name;
You pardoned Magdalen, who wept in shame
Down at Your feet in Simon's dwelling-place;   5700
By wicked Judas we know You were betrayed
For thirty deniers, an evil wage!
Upon the Cross the foul Jews had You nailed
And You bore death so that we might be saved;
On the third day You rose from death again   5705
And broke down, all resistless, Hell's dark gates
And cast Your friends from its infernal jail;
They dwell now in Your mansion, in glory framed;
You rose to Heaven upon Ascension Day;

As truly, Lord, as we believe and state   5710
The truth of all these things I have proclaimed,
Protect, I pray, Lord Oliver the brave
From Charles's nephew Roland's deadly blade!
Fine God, my Lord, through Your most blessèd name,
Make peace between these two and their debate;   5715
If one should die by any stroke of fate,
    Then I, likewise, should perish."

161

Fair-visaged Aude laments — and by her side
Renier the duke and Girart do likewise,
With all of those up in the palace high —   5720
For Oliver, the vassal highly prized,
Who fights against Count Roland for their rights;
The bravest there are filled with dread and fright,
For Roland is a very valiant knight;
But Oliver is brave, and quick and lithe: 5725
He aims a blow at Roland between the eyes,
Which breaks the circle upon the helmet bright
And robs the nasal-knob of a large slice;
Across the thrice-meshed coat the iron glides
And rips off more than sixty rings meanwhile;   5730
Down to the ground the burnished sword-blade drives:
"Most blessèd Mary!" the marquis Roland cries:
"How great a sin! How great a wrong that I
    Should be beset so badly!"

162

Roland the duke is filled with wrath to see   5735
His helmet shorn of its stout nasal-piece
And his strong coat reft of its rings and breached —
More than one hundred rings lie on the field!
With Durendal, which he knows how to wield
Full well, he stalks Count Oliver with zeal;   5740
On his striped helm a mighty blow he deals:
The blade of steel drives downwards and it shears
One hundred rings from his coat's double-seams;

On his left side vermilion blood appears
As Renier's son is forced down to his knees;   5745
He falls with shame — my lords, I guarantee —
And leaps, like a brave man, back to his feet,
In self-defense as fits a warrior fierce;
He calls on God, the Judge of all and each,
To save him here from death and from defeat,   5750
So he may see once more his fearsome breed,
Girart the duke, who did such worthy deeds,
And his fair sister and his father Renier:
"My lord Roland," thus Count Oliver speaks:
"Is that Joyeuse, fierce-visaged Charles's steel,   5755
With which you lay such lusty blows on me?"
"No, my fine lord," Roland the brave repeats:
"It is gold-hilted Durendal you feel,
With which this day I shall bring you to heel
So ruthlessly that Girart's heart will heave   5760
For sending you to battle with me here!"
Says Oliver: "You'll rue it first, indeed!
For it is you who shall this day pay dear,
    If God blesses my weapons!"

163

When Oliver beholds his hauberk torn   5765
And cleft of all its rings by Durendal,
Count Roland's sharp and cutting steel-made sword,
Then his heart grieves and he is angered sore;
With Halteclere, which had no peer before,
He strikes Count Roland's helm so hard once more   5770
That all the garland-stones are struck and shorn;
The blow drives on and strikes his coat of war,
Slicing the skirts, unhindered in its course;
Upon the grassy field the coat-tails fall!
"God!" Roland says, "That was well struck, I'm sure!   5775
His sharp steel blade cuts with a deadly force,
And he himself has strength enough for four!
But I can see he loves me not at all."
Count Oliver hears this and he retorts:
"I hear you very well, Roland my lord;   5780

So help me God, our everlasting Lord,
In all of this your thoughts of me are false!
I did not come to fight you out of choice;
But if it has pleased Jesus, King of us all,
That I have stooped your pride in one small point,
  Then I would be most happy."   5785

164

Upon the isle these two brave lords contend;
There never were two knights of such prowess;
They swap great blows with their blades' cutting edge;
Behold Girart upon his battlements!   5790
The worthy duke speaks out before his men:
"God be your guard, fine nephew Oliver,
By His worthy command, in glory held!
If you defeat this day Duke Roland's strength
And make him yield in honor or in death,   5795
The King's ill-will towards us shall not end
And we shall never make peace with him again!"
Strong Charles, meanwhile, on the plain of Vienne,
Is knelt in prayer in his large, royal tent:
With all his heart he begs Jesus to bless   5800
And guard his nephew Roland whom he loves well,
So that the duke, by yielding or by death,
  Does not meet with dishonor.

165

On foot both knights fight bravely on the field;
Each in his hand bears high his naked steel;   5805
Their armor is so ripped apart and pierced
That it's a wonder they both still live and breathe;
Inside Vienne the sighs and cries are clear
And on the plain the French lament and grieve;
In Charles's host, the King so white of beard,   5810
One hundred knights with no delay or leave
Put on their weapons and armor secretly;
Beneath Vienne, in ambush there concealed,
They lie in wait for Oliver, agreed

To have his head as soon as he appears;   5815
But news of this is brought to Charles's ears;
In heavy rage the King swears by his beard
That there's no lord, however proud a peer,
Whom he'll not hang upon a well-branched tree,
If he commits so foul an infamy;   5820
When they hear this, those ambushers retreat
And watch the duel in silence and in peace,
    Laying aside their weapons.

166

On foot both knights fight fiercely on the isle;
Great blows they swap upon their helmet-stripes   5825
And the sparks fly from their sharp blades of iron;
Both of their shields are reft and cleft aside
And their mail-coats so wrecked and ripped awry
That not even one half of one survives;
At this Sir Roland considers in his mind   5830
How he may test Sir Oliver and try
His loyalty, so praised by other knights:
"Sir Oliver," the fierce-faced Roland cries:
"My body aches, I can no more deny,
And I should like to lie down for a while,   5835
Seeking repose which I greatly require."
"This I regret, lord," Oliver replies:
"For I would rather see this steel blade of mine
Cause you distress than something otherwise;
But, if you wish, attend your need and lie   5840
Upon my shield, whose boards you've broken wide;
And I shall fan you, to cool your body's fire,
Until such time as you feel better, sire."
Roland hears this and marvels in his mind;
With ringing voice he says aloud and high: 5845
"Lord Oliver, your wit is far from wise!
I told a lie to test your loyalty!
I could fight on for four whole days entire
And never think of food and drink the while."
Lord Oliver replies: "And I alike: 5850
So we may recommence our mortal strife."
Roland replies: "Most willingly, say I,

Until tomorrow evening or night!"
Their fearsome swords begin once more to strike,
But their fierce sweat oppresses them so nigh, 5855
Which streams down to their waist on every side,
That they can't wield their weapons true to fight;
When he sees this, Count Roland's rage is wild:
"Sir Oliver," the warrior says, "my eyes
Have never yet beheld so strong a knight, 5860
Who could endure so long the blows I strike!"
"Roland, my lord," Count Oliver replies:
"I know, as long as I am helped by Christ,
That mortal blows are no threat to my life;
　　No man alive can harm me." 5865

167

How hard they fight! How fiercely and how dread
They lunge and plunge and strike with greater strength
Than ever heard of before between two men!
They would not stop and never stint themselves
Till one of them lies on the island dead: 5870
But God shall turn these two foes into friends,
In a strong comradeship that will not end
Until the day it shall be closed and cleft
At Roncevaux, in that desolate realm,
By Ganelon, may Lord God curse the wretch! 5875
He sold them to the Pagan forces there
Of King Marsile, may Jesus curse his breath!
In mighty France no day dawned ever hence
　　When such a loss was suffered!

168

They battle on, they fight each other fiercely 5880
Till daylight fades and it is nearly evening;
They're in no mood for halting then or yielding,
Both spurred along by anger and ill-feeling,
With naked blades firm in their hands for wielding;
Each would fight on and sell his honor dearly, 5885
When a thick cloud falls from the sky between them,
Forming a mist which stops each knight from seeing;

They make no sound and make no movement either,
The braver there filled with alarm and fearful,
And they are certain that death is coming near them;   5890
Then from the cloud an Angel steps, who sweetly
In Lord God's name addresses them and greets them:
"My noble knights, you have been honored deeply!
This feud and fight of yours no more shall be, lords;
Not one more blow must be exchanged, for Jesus   5895
The Lord our God forbids you to proceed it!
Henceforth in Spain against the race of heathens
Your fierce prowess shall yet be known and needed;
Men shall know well your valor there and see it
      In service of God's love."   5900

169

Both of the knights are very much afraid
To hear the will of the Lord God proclaimed;
The Angel says: "My lords, be not dismayed!
From high in Heaven God urges you this day:
Let be this rivalry of clan and claim!   5905
In hostile land upon the heathen race,
There you may prove who is or is not brave;
Throughout the realm of King Marsile of Spain,
There you may win his kingdom with your blades
Out of the hands of his Saracen knaves,   5910
And glorify God's faith and His own name;
And your reward for this shall be most great:
Your souls shall earn true pardon and true grace;
In Heaven high, in His great dwelling-place,
      God shall set them in glory."   5915

170

When both the knights have heard the Angel's speech,
Forbidding them to fight by God's decree,
The Glorious one, the King of Majesty,
They say: "True King of Heaven, may You be
Adored as Lord and God of all and each,   5920
Since you have sent your messenger and made clear
Your will by word of Your own Angel here!"

The Angel does not tarry now but leaves,
And the two counts waste no more time indeed;
The Holy Spirit has filled them with new zeal; 5925
They rest themselves beneath a well-branched tree
And there they pledge in love and loyalty
Their comradeship to last their lifelong years;
Roland speaks forth, whose courage is most fierce:
"Lord Oliver, this I will not conceal: 5930
I pledge to you all of my loyalty;
I love you more than any man that breathes,
Save Charles, who is my strong and royal liege;
Since God decrees that we should be at peace,
There is no fort henceforth or town I'll seize, 5935
No tower or city, nor any castle-keep,
That I'll not share with you, if you agree;
I shall wed Aude, if you give her to me,
And if I may, before four days have been,
I shall unite King Charles and you in peace; 5940
But if he turns a deaf ear to my pleas
And still refuses friendship, then I shall leave
And come to you within the town in brief;
Then all his life this quarrel shall not cease."
When Oliver hears this, his thanks are deep; 5945
He clasps his hands towards Lord God and speaks:
"Glorious Father, praised be Your name and deeds,
Who have this day allied this man to me!
Roland, my lord, I shall no more conceal:
I love you more than any man that breathes; 5950
I give my sister to you most willingly,
Upon this understanding that you shall hear:
That Vienne's rift with Charles be truly healed!
Now lord, unlace your jeweled helm of green,
So we may kiss in sign of friendship sealed." 5955
The duke replies: "Willingly I agree."
They bare their heads of helms immediately
And kiss each other's cheek most willingly;
Then they sit down upon the grassy field
And pledge faith to each other most loyally, 5960
And comradeship to last their lifelong years;
  Thus peace was made between them.

Part Four:
The Reconciliation

171

When both the knights have acted in this way,
They kiss once more and then they separate,
Close comrades now until their dying day;   5965
The French see this and they fill with dismay,
And France's Emperor looks on the same;
He calls on God, Who never lies or fails:
"Glorious Lord, by Your mercy and grace,
I never saw a vow like this exchanged: 5970
My own nephew whom in my house I've raised,
Has kissed the man whom I am bound to hate!
I greatly fear he has betrayed my faith
And shamed himself and done his honor blame;
If this is true, he has played me more base   5975
Than Judas did when Jesus was betrayed."
Says Ganelon: "He's done it for Aude's sake,
Whom he adores — this is the truth I state;
He has made peace like this for Aude the maid!"
Naimes hears this and comes to them in haste;   5980
He speaks aloud for Charles to hear and says:
"Do not dismay, true Emperor Charlemagne!
Let the good, valiant count come and explain;
Then you will know what pledges have been made
    To warrant this close friendship."   5985

172

"True Emperor," says Naimes the strong knight:
"Let your nephew explain when he arrives!

What do you know of the thoughts in his mind?
By the blest Saint whom sinners seek to find,
I would stand trial of judgement by the fire   5990
Or fight against an Emir to deny
That Duke Roland could have betrayed you, Sire;
He would not do it for all of Milan's might."
Roland himself heads for the Frenchmen's lines;
He sails the stream and from the barge he strides;   5995
They lead him forth a palfrey-horse to ride,
Which by its silver stirrup the duke bestrides;
He rides in haste and in the camp alights —
And many a knight greets him with happy smiles,
    All overjoyed to see him.   6000

173

Roland the duke has left the isle, where he
And Oliver have fought with utmost zeal;
Their shields are split from edge to edge and breached,
Their lances cleft and their sharp-pointed spears;
Their helmet-rings are crushed about their ears;   6005
They have laid low and slain their warring-steeds
With lusty blows of their sharp blades of steel;
Before his tent, beneath a well-leafed tree,
Bides Charles with ten score lords whom he holds dear;
For both knights' sake they fervently beseech   6010
God in His strength to save them from defeat;
Before them all Roland dismounts his steed
And thirty run to help disarm him here;
The Emperor moves up to him and leads
Full many a lord who greets him with good cheer;   6015
Says Charlemagne: "Welcome, my nephew sweet!
You have fought there for a long time indeed!
And Lord Girart — does he not come to yield?
Will he give you Vienne, his palace steep?"
Duke Roland says: "I have not heard him speak;   6020
No word of that was spoken where I've been;
But everyone, bearded and bald, agrees
That your own pride began all of this grief;
Let us ride home; we shall gain no more here!

True Emperor, if you pay heed to me,   6025
Girart shall be a friend you can hold dear,
And we may ride back home to France in brief."
When Charles hears this, his rage is dark and deep;
He looks at him and thinks his wits are weak:
"Fool!" says the King, "How ill you have served me!   6030
Have you defeated Oliver? Where is he?"
"I have not beaten him at all, my liege:
For the Lord God decreed it not to be!
One of His Angels forbade me to proceed,
In a large cloud which hid the count from me;   6035
I tell you truly, Oliver has no peer:
There is no man, however strong, he fears;
Against my blows he stood there proud and fierce
And paid me back whatever he received!
I have endured such great blows from his steel   6040
That will still cause me pain for seven years!"
Inside Vienne Count Oliver retreats
And all the knights greet him as he appears:
Milon of Puglia and Hernaut white of beard,
Geneva's Renier and wise Aymeri   6045
Welcome him back with great delight indeed;
They help him to disarm with every speed:
They lift his helm of beaten gold and seize
Straight off his back his coat of close-meshed weave;
Upon his side the wound is wide and deep: 6050
Guibourc sees it and grieves most heavily;
But there was never a woman as wise as she:
She had some ointment, which Our Lord had bequeathed,
And on his side and trunk she rubs the cream;
Straightway he's better than he has ever been!   6055
They lead him then inside the palace steep,
    Where fair Aude runs towards him.

174

Inside Vienne how joyful are the knights
For Oliver, who has returned alive
From the fierce fight he's fought upon the isle;   6060
And when the count comes in the palace high,

His sister Aude runs up and hugs him tight;
And Roland comes to Charles's tent meanwhile,
Where Charles addresses him and thus enquires:
"My nephew sweet, how has your fortune thrived?   6065
Where now is Oliver the brave and wise?
Have you defeated him? Come, do not hide!"
"No I have not, nor should you think so, Sire!
You have no man who could defeat that knight;
He has made peace with me, thanks be to Christ!   6070
Back to Vienne unharmed he has retired;
Through his blest Angel Lord God forbade us fight;
If he had not, one of us would have died."
"Then God be praised for that," King Charles replies:
"For one hundred gold marks I'd not have liked   6075
Lord Oliver to lose a limb or life."
At this, each one leaves for his rest that night,
Until the morning with the new dawning's light;
The Emperor gets up as dawn arrives
And the good King goes to the church and shrine   6080
To hear the Mass with a true heart and mind;
When Mass is said, the service read and signed,
Out of the church the worthy Emperor strides
And to the door of his own tent retires;
His nephew Roland exhorts him in this wise: 6085
"Uncle," he says, "give ear to me a while!
You have besieged this city with great might
For more than seven years since we arrived;
The Pagans built these walls so strong and high
That no steel pick of ours or bar of iron   6090
Can prise one single building-brick aside,
They are secured so solidly and tight;
And the Rhône river flows fleet and fiercely by!
One score and seven years could run their time
Before you take the strongholds you desire;   6095
Instead of this, make peace with Girart, Sire!"
"You waste your breath!" the Emperor replies:
"I'll not return to France in all my life
Till Vienne falls and its walls lay in piles!
And woe to all whom I may seize inside: 6100
Not one of them shall keep his limbs or life!"

Roland replies: "In thought your threats are high;
But how your deeds match up will show in time;
There is one thing you can be sure of, Sire —
You'll not have me with my sword at my side!"   6105
On hearing this Charles fills with grief and cries:
"Give ear to me a while, my nephew fine!
I know full well, Roland, what has transpired!
When, bearing arms, you went out to the isle
Whence you have just returned after your fight,   6110
I was quite sure you would uphold my right;
But for fair Aude you have been reconciled
With Oliver, whose glove you bear in sign."
"You speak nothing but truth," Roland replies:
"Count Oliver is a most noble knight,   6115
Handsome, well-bred and skillful in a fight;
You could not find three men of France his like!
To win a friend is a most worthy prize!
If he and I can now be reconciled,
Then Girart and yourself can be likewise;   6120
For by the Saint they seek in Rome to find,
I shall not gird my sword to help you, Sire."
"I shall not ask you, wretch!" the Emperor cries:
"Ride from my ranks, for you have too much pride!"
"I shall not, Sire," the noble Roland cries: 6125
"I shall not leave as long as you abide,
But I shall see how you will prosper, Sire,
      With Girart of Vienne."

175

My worthy lords, you all have heard it well,
Each one of you, young-bloods and hoary-heads: 6130
King Charles's rage at Girart was so dread
That he besieged him for seven years on end
With four more kings and fourteen dukes of wealth
And thirty counts of mighty power and strength;
The other force could not be reckoned less   6135
Than four times forty thousand brave knights and men;
The rearguard troops of France arrive at length
And see the siege-machines and mangonels;
Girart himself stands at a window's ledge,

The coat of mail he wears bruising his flesh; 6140
Lady Guibourc is standing by him there:
A lovelier wife no king or duke possessed;
She looks at him and speaks aloud and says:
"How is it with you now, my noble friend?
Are you defeated, then — is this well said? 6145
For white-haired Charles has held you so hard-pressed,
And has laid waste so widely to your realm
That for ten leagues a steed could run unchecked
And not find wheat enough in all that length
To feed one horse from dawn until day's end! 6150
If you had done as I advised you best,
Your realm would not be wasted now and bled,
Nor would this allod, this conquest of Vienne,
Be taken as the King's or tendered yet."
Count Oliver comes up, when this is said; 6155
   And they will speak together.

176

Maytime it is, with roses on the thorn;
The oriole sings out, the blackbird calls;
The woodlands bloom, the grass is green once more,
And every flood flows back into its course; 6160
And every lover for his beloved is fraught
And often sighs when of his love forlorn;
King Charlemagne, whose beard with age is hoar,
Bides in his tent of Spanish silk before
The well-stocked walls of Vienne town and fort, 6165
With all his knights around him and his lords;
Both kings and counts are in his mighty force,
Princes and dukes and all the knights they've brought;
And many a baron bides in his entourage:
"Lord God," he says, "Who governs each and all; 6170
Glorious Father, of blessèd Mary born,
I have defeated seven great kings in war;
By force of arms and courage I have forced
Each one of them to serve me and my cause;
Each one of them obeys my will and voice 6175
And holds from me whatever he enjoys;

Yet here I see a duke whose claim is small,
Whose holding here runs in my realm and law,
Yet he serves me with not the smallest coin!
I'd rather die than leave him in his hall!"   6180
Richard the duke of Normandy speaks forth:
"True Emperor, do not dismay at all!
Have it announced within these well-stocked walls
To Duke Girart, who flouts you with such gall,
That he must cede this ancient town of yours   6185
With all its towers and all its wealth and stores,
And he and all his breed must heed your law!
By Jesus Christ, should he refuse your call,
Then turn your siege into a fierce assault!
The French are fierce and valiant with their swords   6190
In daring deeds and in the ways of war:
From Vienne field, while some besiege the walls,
We shall attack time and again in force;
While they're alive we never shall withdraw
Until the town and all within it fall!   6195
Seize forth Girart to punish in accord
With judgement passed by all your mighty lords!"
King Charles responds, whose beard and hair are hoar:
"Richard of Normandy, well said, my lord!"
Inside Vienne, within its vaulted hall,   6200
Abides Girart, the valiant-visaged lord,
While at his side stands his duchess Guibourc;
She says to him, as a wise wife well ought:
"For the blest Son of Mary's sake, my lord,
Take counsel now, my fierce-faced, fine Girart,   6205
Of all the barons and all these knights of yours
Within this land which has been so destroyed
And in this town so long besieged by war;
This foolishness has cost too dearly, for
From Burgundy to here and furthermore   6210
To Lombardy your land is scarred and scorched;
Make peace with Charles for God's sake, I implore!"
Then says the valiant-visaged Lord Oliver:
"You speak the truth, noble Lady Guibourc;
If my uncle permits, let us speak more   6215
    With Hernaut of Biaulande."

177

Lords, at this time of which my tale recites,
Vienne contained two palaces of might:
The poorer one was rich enough, you'd find!
And in the one bearded Hernaut abides 6220
While in the other lives Lord Girart the wise;
There is no man on earth who could contrive
To list their excellence or to describe
The wealth their marble walls contained inside;
Lady Guibourc of noble form and fine, 6225
Steps down the marble stones and goes outside;
Along the streets of Vienne town she strides
Until she comes to that palace which I
Have told you of, where wise Hernaut resides;
She mounts the steps into the hall and finds 6230
Lord Hernaut there, so fine and feared a knight,
And he is playing at backgammon and dice;
He stands straight up when he sees her arrive,
And with his right arm round her neck entwined
He asks: "My lady, do you seek help of mine? 6235
What is your need? Do not hide your desire!"
"My lord," she says, "I shall speak out my mind:
Great is the siege which has been set outside,
And it has lasted for seven years entire!
King Charles is there, the strong and royal, beside 6240
All of his knights, you know this is no lie;
Now he has called his French rearguard to fight;
There is no man of woman born to life,
Save clerks or priests ordained in Jesus Christ,
Who has not come to join his army's lines; 6245
And maidens too of noble form and fine
To whom he gives rich husbands from his knights;
They will stay here all the days of their lives
Till our walls fall and Vienne is on fire!
Girart my lord will lose his limbs and life 6250
If he is caught and made captive inside,
And you will too, be certain, and likewise
Milon of Puglia and brave Renier the wise,
And Aymeri, the youth well-praised and prized,
And Oliver, fearless and feared alike; 6255

And both my sons shall lose their own birthright,
Beuvon the elder and Savariez likewise;
And I shall be the butt of shame and gibe."
"You speak the truth, my lady," Hernaut replies:
"But I shall do whatever you desire;   6260
Though all my deeds earned shame in others' eyes,
I would still act out of my love for Christ
And for you, lady, if you bid me to strike."
"My lord," she says, "God bless and let you thrive!"   6265
They leave the hall and down the steps they stride,
And through the streets on foot they wend and wind;
They meet Girart, the duke of noble line,
Who from his marble hall has stepped alike;
    Now they will speak together.   6270

178

While Girart greets his worthy wife and speaks
With his brother Hernaut, the brave and fierce,
Behold Renier arrive with Moreheier;
Count Oliver is also there with these,
Keen to arrange a peace with utmost speed;   6275
And an accord would soon have been agreed
By envoys sent to sue the French for peace,
Had it not been for haughty Aymeri:
As evening comes he rides off with his spear
To Charles's tent and slays his counsellor   6280
And Guielin his treasurer-in-chief;
When he sees this, Charles fills with rage and grief;
He calls aloud: "Knights, after him! If he
Escapes you here, your names will be held cheap!"
When this is said, they do not curb their zeal,   6285
And Aymeri, without delay, retreats!
Three hundred knights give chase and threaten each
To hew his head with their stout swords of steel!
Right to the Rhône they ride hot on his heels;
But Aymeri, once there, leaps off his steed   6290
Straight in a boat where fourteen sailors heave
Upon the oars to take him through the stream;
Right to Vienne their labors do not cease;

Up to the hall he climbs the stairway steep;
Girart moves up, enraged, when he appears,   6295
And says: "You wretch, God damn you for your deeds!
Why did you go to Charles, bearing your spear?
By doing this you have put back the peace
Which we this day have chosen to achieve;
We were about to give an envoy leave   6300
To sue for peace and have it signed and sealed!"
When this is said, a messenger appears
Whose wont had been to spy on the French peers;
And he has heard the news with his own ears
That Charles intends to go out hunting deer;   6305
He sees the count and calls aloud and clear:
"My lord Girart, and you, my lord Renier,
And you, Hernaut, lord of Biaulande the fierce:
You used to be brave knights and were more feared
Than any storm and any lightning-streak!   6310
But now the French don't fear you in the least —
Their fiery steeds are grazing in your fields!
Tomorrow Charles will go out hunting here
Within Clermont your forest wide and deep;
No more than seven knights with him he'll keep: 6315
Duke Otto of Bavaria there'll be
With Didier the Lombard of Pavie,
And with these two the rich Duke Gaifier;
So help me God the Father, none of these three
Has one whole denier's worth of bravery   6320
To save himself or help one more in need!"
Girart hears this and fills with joyful cheer;
The counts take counsel on it and soon agree:
"Barons, my lords, prepare at once to leave!
If we cannot avenge the shame we feel,   6325
Cursed be the hand that gives us food to eat!"
Some twenty knights make ready with all speed;
They don their coats and lace their helms of steel;
On their left hip they gird their swords, then leap
Into the saddle of their good warring-steeds;   6330
Around their necks they hang their quartered shields
And in their hands they grip strong, cutting spears;
They light bright candles in noble holders reared

And ride inside a tunnel dug underneath
The city gates by Pagans of bygone years;   6335
Its walls are whiter than snow upon a beach;
All twenty knights ride in there on their steeds
And leave the city, riding beneath the streets
Until, just shortly before the dawn appears,
They see Berart the woodsman's dwelling near;   6340
It is his duty to guard the forest's reach;
All of their horses they leave beneath some trees
To graze the grass and cool down in the breeze;
They clutch their spears and climb a laurel-tree;
When morning comes with sunlight bright and clear   6345
The King gets up, puts on his hunting-gear
And a great pair of boots upon his feet;
His horn is brought, his hounds put on the leash;
He mounts his horse, as do his knights, and leaves
Upon the hunt deep in the forest green;   6350
Without God's help no coming back there'll be
    For Emperor Charlemagne.

179

The Emperor arrives in Clermont forest;
He unleashes his hounds and they plunge forward;
They start a boar, a fearsome beast and awful;   6355
The greyhounds yelp and raise the hunt there for it;
With all their strength the huntsmen close the boar then
And Charles the King, upon a long-maned palfrey,
Outruns them all, the bearded and the bald ones;
But then the King meets with a great misfortune: 6360
His men lose sight of him across a moorland
And they don't know which way their hunt has brought them;
Along a path, an ancient and a worn one,
The boar escapes and the dogs chase undaunted,
With Charles, as soon as he sees where, on horseback   6365
In hot pursuit until the beast is cornered;
Beneath a tree, beside a fount of water,
The boar has stopped to make a stand before them;
Charles looks at it and lighting from his palfrey
He strikes the boar like a strong man and stalwart   6370

Till it is slain with his well-tempered sword-blade;
He draws a knife and cutting out the offal
He throws it down to his hounds to reward them;
He's kept his horn and blows it now, rejoicing;
And that Berart, the woodsman of the forest,   6375
Has stalked the King so closely all that morning
That any move he made this Berart saw it!
Now he rides off to Girart without pausing
And just as soon as he sees him, he calls him:
"Fine duke, my lord, do not dismay at all, sire!   6380
I have pursued the King of France so surely
That I know all about his morning's fortune!
Hard by a fount a wild-boar he's slaughtered
Beneath a tree, where now, alone, he pauses!
He has with him no young or older courtiers,   6385
For all his men have lost him in the forest!
None of them know where he has gone before them!
Girart, fine duke, why do you stay or dawdle?
Without a shield or spear Charles may be caught now
    And made to pay your price!"   6390

180

The valiant knights, when they hear Berart speak,
With one accord and voice cry all and each:
"My lords, to horse, by blessèd St. Denis!"
And so they mount, none loth but willingly:
"Make haste to ride!" cries out fierce Aymeri,   6395
And they set off among those well-leafed trees
With good Berart to guide them and to lead;
Charles takes no care, not ware that they are near
Till from all sides he is enclosed and seized
By the rein-straps of his Arabian steed;   6400
Duke Girart knows how brave the King can be
And in great haste he takes his burnished spear,
And then he says: "Sir King, see Girart here!
You thought that I would still be fast asleep
Inside Vienne, with hunger wan and weak!   6405
But no, I'm very much awake indeed!
You blew your horn and we heard loud and clear,

And every word you've said has reached our ears!
This boar is mine, you've slain it wrongfully!
And now my knights shall have it served to eat,   6410
As will my wife, of form so fair and sweet;
And you, my lord, shall come back home with me!"
Says Aymeri: "Fine uncle, kill him here!
Cut off his head right now with your sharp steel,
And then this war and this dispute may cease!"   6415
Girart replies: "May God forbid the deed!
A King of France shall not be harmed by me!
If he forgives me, I'll be his man of liege
And hold from him all of my lands in fief;
If he will not, by blessèd St. Maurice,   6420
I shall depart for Arab lands and leave;
I shall be shamed and men shall lose esteem
    For our Emperor's honor."

181

When Charlemagne hears Girart's frank reply,
Who in good faith seeks pardon of his Sire,   6425
Not deeming him his captive or his prize,
Then he looks up towards the sky four times:
"Ah God, the King of everyone," he cries:
"Such miracles for me You have contrived!
This war against Girart of Vienne shire   6430
I dreaded more than any other strife!
God curse me now, if I pursue the fight!
Come forward, Duke Girart, you worthy knight!"
"What do you want?" noble Girart inquires;
The King replies: "I shall reveal my mind: 6435
Peace shall be yours in such terms as you like,
And in sweet France you shall have your desire;
I pardon you the payment of my fines
And I grant you each third coin of my rights;
Those whom you love I shall welcome likewise,   6440
And those you hate I shall likewise despise."
"May God forbid," well-bred Girart replies:
"That you should lose part of your wealth for mine;

Hernaut my brother, who is older than I,
Should be called lord before me at all times."   6445
Then Hernaut kneels before the King and plights
His loyal word to be his man for life,
And then Girart of Vienne does alike;
Milon of Puglia responds in kind,
With Oliver the brave and courtly knight;   6450
No fiercer heart than Aymeri's you'd find:
All of this time he has stood on one side,
Watching them all, to judge the wrong and right
Of the amends they make to Charles's might:
"Vassal," says Charles, "and what is your reply?   6455
Will you make peace or war with me and mine?"
"Truly, I do not know," the youth replies:
"I see my father and uncle with my own eyes
Caught in your trap like young birds in the lime —
I who cried out to hew your head erstwhile   6460
Must earn the curse of everyone in Christ!
But since you have these others tamed and tied,
I have no wish to stand alone and fight;
Whatever they say, I'll hold with and comply;
I shall serve you as my duty requires,   6465
And when I have, I shall observe you, Sire;
If you reward me, your own gain shall be high."
"You speak well, friend," the King of France replies:
"Both Oliver and you shall be my knights:
With my nephew Sir Roland, three of a kind,   6470
You'll bear the Oriflamme when we must fight."
"Much thanks, Lord King," young Aymeri replies:
"Wretch! On your knees before him!" Duke Girart cries:
"Can you not see his love for you is kind?"
Says Aymeri: "My lord, you do not lie."   6475
He moves to kneel before his King, contrite,
But Charles draws him towards him and helps him rise;
Hernaut speaks out: "What will you do now, Sire?
Will you go to your camp or at our side
Be honored in Vienne when we arrive?   6480
Let Alemans and Germans hear it cried
    That Charles has Vienne city!"

182

Hernaut speaks out: "Good King, listen to me:
Will you go to your camp or with us here
Be honored in Vienne when you appear?   6485
If we should ride into your host at siege
Before the French have had the truth revealed
Of our accord and how we have made peace,
We should be slain and slaughtered all and each!"
The King replies: "You speak the truth, indeed."   6490
"True Emperor," wise-witted Girart speaks:
"Ere evening comes we'll ride, if you agree,
Down underground upon our warring-steeds
Along a passage of great antiquity
Which leads straight to my wondrous city's streets;   6495
The Pagans dug this tunnel in bygone years."
The King replies: "Fine duke, just as you please;
But sir, beware of any treachery!"
The duke replies: "You speak madly, my liege;
Though I lost limb, I would not use deceit."   6500
When this is said, they spur into the deep;
The forester Berart was wise indeed:
Bearing a lantern he lights them in the lead
As underground they journey on their steeds;
Wise-witted Charles marvels beyond belief;   6505
He sees Girart and asks as they proceed:
"Fine Duke Girart, my lord, listen to me!
I've won in war so many towns and keeps
And all the land from here to Balaguer;
But such a tunnel or road I've never seen!   6510
For seven years we have maintained our siege
And never knew this passage-way was here!
We could have stayed another seven years
Before our hands or hunger made you yield!"
Girart replies: "In all your life, my liege,   6515
You'd not have forced us from our castle-keep:
For I would leave my city by this means
To hunt my boars and my fat woodland deer
And bring back wealth from foreign realms and fiefs
Which I would give to Vienne generously   6520
So all would be well nourished and live at ease."

"In truth," says Charles, "you would, I do believe!"
When this is said, they come to Vienne's streets;
In the town square, beneath two well-branched trees,
The King dismounts with all the knights, who lead   6525
Him to the hall with marble walls agleam,
Where he is served with honor joyfully;
Lady Guibourc, of noble form and sweet,
And lovely Aude, with beauty rare replete,
Return at once from prayer at St. Maurice,   6530
Where they have stayed a long time on their knees
Beseeching God, the King of Majesty,
To save Girart the wise duke from defeat,
And all the knights he led beneath the streets
Along the tunnel into the woodland green;   6535
Lady Guibourc is wise of wit indeed;
She sees the King and knows him when she sees
His face and nose, and look which is so fierce,
And by his brow which is lofty and clear;
She sees Girart and thus directs her speech: 6540
"Fine duke, where did you find this King, tell me?
For God's sake do not treat him with cruelty,
Neither do anything which may displease!
Submit yourself instead at Charles's feet
And give him back Vienne as his own fief."   6545
"Lady," he answers, "your speech is in arrears!
Since morn this day I've done as he bade me;
I have become his man and vassal here,
With homage done and pledge of fealty,
As have all of my brothers whom here you see."   6550
"God," says Guibourc, "may You be praised indeed!
Whoever hosts King Charles for one night here
Within Vienne and serves him honorably,
Will raise the honor of all their family."
Girart says: "Lady, you have my happy leave   6555
    To render him this service."

183

Listen, my lords, may Lord God bless and keep you!
Not everyone knows well the song you're hearing!

Some singers have not learnt or kept the details
Of the true tale that you have heard from me here: 6560
How Charlemagne the Emperor white-bearded
Was captured as he hunted in the greenwood,
Like a bird in a cage, and led in secret
By Duke Girart back to Vienne the fearful;
The day he came, how joyful was the cheering   6565
Of all the knights and all the common people;
Lady Guibourc comes forward now to meet him
And, seeing him, gives him a noble greeting;
Nobody saw before so great a feasting
As Charlemagne the King receives that evening!   6570
He does not get a lonely cell to sleep in:
Both high and low wait on him well between them;
But all the honor that Charlemagne receives here
Is quite unknown to all those in the siege-host;
Those who went off to hunt in the dense greenwood   6575
With Charlemagne the Emperor white-bearded,
When they at length can neither see nor hear him,
Turn in their tracks and to their tents go speeding;
The siege-host knights come forward there to meet them,
Asking for Charles, of blessèd France the leader: 6580
"Barons, my lords," says Naimes the white-bearded:
"Cursed be this land and realm today, by Jesus!
The hills are high, the rocks are sharp and piercing,
The valleys long and overgrown the greenwood;
When Charles startled his prey among the trees there,   6585
A boar or a fat sow or some such creature,
He gave pursuit till he could kill and keep it;
Since he rode off, we've neither heard nor seen him,
Nor do we know which way he took when leaving;
If he has met with people of the region   6590
Whose mighty lands he has taken in seizure,
They will avenge themselves with every evil!"
When they all hear of Charles's disappearance,
My lords, you never saw such bitter grieving!
Such great dismay besets all in the siege-host   6595
That all that night nobody drinks or eats there
Or lifts a saddle from any war-horse either;
Until next day, with light of dawn appearing,

All of the knights and all the common people
    Lament King Charlemagne.   6600

184

Barons and counts, knights, men-at-arms the same
Throughout the host are filled with great dismay
For their rich King, the mighty Charlemagne,
Whose whereabouts they do not know or fate;
And yet their valiant Emperor is safe   6605
And at great ease inside Vienne the great:
He is well served by counts of noble rate,
By Duke Girart and all those of his race;
Before the King so rich a feast is laid
And such bright flares light up the hall of state   6610
That none before ever saw so fine a blaze!
I'll not describe the rich dishes displayed:
Each has as much as appetite can crave;
And so much wine, claret and spiced, is drained,
That to describe it would be a weary tale!   6615
With Charles his guest Girart takes every pain:
He serves the food himself on Charles's plate,
Whose silver cup is borne by Oliver;
The other counts sit at his side in wait:
The count Hernaut, lord of Biaulande the great,   6620
And brave Geneva's lord, Count Renier,
And Count Milon of Puglia, ever brave;
Young Aymeri serves all the nobles there;
Lady Guibourc, of heart and courage great,
Sits on the other side of Charlemagne   6625
With lovely Aude, so fair of form and face:
The palace glows with her beauty and grace;
The King looks at the maid time and again,
Then calls Girart and says with his voice raised:
"Fine duke, my lord, hear what I have to say: 6630
I ask of you to give me this fair maid,
Whom I would give in marriage as a mate
To my own nephew Roland, who is more brave
And better than any knight alive today;
Together they will make a perfect pair."   6635

Says Girart: "Lord, your wish I shall obey;
Do as you will and whatever you may."
Before them all he gives his glove in gage,
And Charles the King returns his thanks the same;
When all the knights have eaten, servants make haste   6640
With squires there to clear the cloths away;
They all make merry throughout the hall of state
As tales are told and the viele is played,
Then all retire to sleep until dawn breaks;
Inside a room of great beauty they place   6645
The mighty Emperor King Charlemagne,
Inside a bed more lovely and ornate
Than ever where a count or emir lay;
If those French knights who now bemoan his fate
Could know how well he fares in Girart's care,   6650
Then most would be much more at ease, I'd say,
For Charlemagne of heart and courage great
Is sleeping now at utmost ease and safe
Inside Vienne until the dawn of day;
When morning comes, before the sun's first rays,   6655
The knights arise and foot-soldiers the same;
Naimes the duke, whose hair and beard are gray,
With Roland and three thousand, make their way
Throughout the forest in search of Charlemagne,
Down every ridge and valley that it contains;   6660
When they do not find Charles, their grief is great
And they return heart-sick in their dismay;
But in Vienne the hearts are light and gay,
To have great Charles in their own hall of state;
The King arises when he sees the dawn break;   6665
Girart the duke and his brave baronage
All come before the mighty Charlemagne
And greet him fair in our Redeemer's name;
Then they all go to the chapel in haste,
Where bishop Morant sings Mass for their souls' sake,   6670
And they give coins and silks of gold inlay;
When Mass is said, they do not stop or wait:
King Charlemagne and Duke Girart the brave
Mount on the backs of their good destriers
And take with them two thousand in their train;   6675

They all are dressed as finely as they may
In costly robes and garments richly made;
Bearing no arms, in a joyful parade
    They ride from Vienne city.

185

King Charlemagne of fierce temper and strength,   6680
With Duke Girart, his closest lords and friends,
Rides from Vienne in great joy and content:
Without lances or shields two thousand men;
With hue and cry they show their happiness
As they ride straight towards the host of French;   6685
Naimes the duke and Roland see them ahead
And the siege-host fills with an awful dread;
The boldest there fills with foreboding then:
"My lords," says Naimes, "evil rests on our heads,
Since we have lost great Charles our Emperor!   6690
Behold what force has ridden from Vienne:
It is Girart with all his lords and friends
Come here in strength to send us to our deaths!
They must have learnt that we have been bereft
Of Charlemagne, lost by our foolishness."   6695
When they hear this, the French fill with distress;
They seize their arms, the great ones and the less,
And mount their swift and long-maned destriers,
Sounding their horns with long and lusty breath;
When all are armed, both young and old, they head   6700
Their destriers towards King Charles himself!
When he sees this, the Emperor laughs, and then
He calls Girart, who rides beside him there:
"Fine duke, my lord, we have frightened my men!
They come at us in full armor and strength!   6705
By Jesus Christ, if it were our intent
To swap hard blows, then we could do it well!
They do not know how things have changed for them;
I shall ride forth till they see me at length!"
Then he spurs forth his long-maned destrier   6710
And leaves behind the company he's kept;
He meets Naimes and Roland, whom he loves best,

And when these two behold their liege again
They feel more joy than either ever felt!
Each one dismounts his horse at once and steps   6715
Towards his lord and lifts his pointed helm:
"My lords, fear not," says Charles, "neither be vexed!
You have no need to summon all these men;
Thanks be to God our cause has prospered well —
For now we have the prize of our long quest: 6720
Girart and I are allies now and friends,
    And our feuding has finished."

186

When all the knights hear Charlemagne's own voice
Tell them that he has reached a peace accord
With Duke Girart, whose many blows they've borne,   6725
They feel such joy as none had felt before;
Each one calls out: "Praised be the God our Lord,
And bless the man whose hand has stopped this war;
Now we may go back to our homes and halls
Which we've not seen for seven years or more."   6730
When this is said, they ride back one and all,
Where they dismount and lay aside their swords;
King Charles dismounts before his great tent's door,
Then calls his knights, his princes and his lords;
He mounts his folding-stool and, standing tall,   6735
He looks at them and thus he speaks to all:
"Attend to me," he says, "barons, my lords:
You know it well, I went out yestermorn
As one of seven to hunt game in Clermont;
Deep in the forest I chased a fearsome boar,   6740
And when I'd struck him with my nielloed point,
Girart arrived with his fierce kin in force!
I thought my death or agony assured;
But such an humble grace to me he bore,
That at my feet he knelt down and implored   6745
Mercy of me in his wisdom of thought,
As did Hernaut, that brave and famous lord;
When I saw this, my pity grew for all:
For they had caught me and I was in their thrall!
I pardoned them with good will and with joy: 6750

I've never seen such loyalty before;
Now I ask you for your advice, my lords:
What means have I to recompense them for
This realm of theirs wasted by us in war?"
Naimes replies: "Your words are wise, my lord;   6755
So help me God, I've told you once and more
That you were very wrong towards Girart;
So help me God, if your amends fall short,
You'll have no more my friendship or support."
"Naimes," says Charles, "you speak as wisdom ought;   6760
My lord Girart, come forward now!" he calls:
"I give this land to you freely henceforth,
And in sweet France you shall keep all that's yours;
Those whom you love shall be loved in my court
And those you hate shall likewise be abhorred,   6765
Stripped of their lands and leave my palace poor!"
Girart replies: "My grateful thanks, my lord."
From his tall height at Charles's feet he falls,
Who with Naimes raises him from the floor;
Throughout the land the word is cried and called   6770
That Charles will leave the region and withdraw,
And that whoever among the Emperor's force
Will lose by this even two denier coins,
Shall be repaid four times the loss henceforth;
And then the merchants who have brought goods and stores   6775
Begin to sell the merchandise they've brought:
From the next morning, as soon as day has dawned,
Until the evening and darkness starts to fall,
They do not cease their going back and forth
Until the town is bursting with them all!   6780
Down in the fields they lodge outside the walls,
Where they pitch tents and shelters of all sorts;
All of the knights and peers are filled with joy
And clerks and priests and tonsured monks rejoice
    That peace is sworn between them.   6785

187

Maytime it is, aglow with warmth and peace,
The trees in leaf and green upon the fields,

And maids content who have their lovers near!
The birds are singing most beautifully and clear;
Upon a feast-day of my lord St. Maurice,   6790
King Charles holds court more nobly than I've seen,
Inside Vienne in a great hall replete
With many a knight of highest bravery;
They are well served with richest foods and meats,
And afterwards, before the barons leave,   6795
Lady Guibourc comes from a room and leads
By her right hand young Aude so fair and sweet;
Clad in a silken robe of peerless sheen,
Her beauty makes the palace glow and gleam;
Those who see her are dazzled by what they see: 6800
"God," says King Charles, "how fair a maid is she!"
Hernaut replies: "Fine lord, she is indeed;
You know in truth that she is my own niece,
The daughter of the noble Count Renier
And sister of Count Oliver the fierce."   6805
King Charles responds: "Give this fair maid to me,
For Roland's sake, he whom I hold most dear;
No other man I ask her for but he;
When he weds her no day can ever cleave
The bond between both of our families;   6810
And if the Lord, Who never lies, decrees
By His own grace that an heir be conceived,
What good may come in time from his great deeds!"
Hernaut replies: "Just as you wish, my liege;
My niece could never wed a higher peer   6815
    Than one of your own kindred."

188

Up on his feet stands fierce-faced Charlemagne;
He calls his nephew, for whom his love is great,
And gives him Aude to be his wife and mate;
Taking her hand, the King gives her away   6820
In view of all his knights and baronage;
And the Archbishop bears witness there the same,
Before them all declaring Aude engaged;
They name the day the wedding shall take place —

Princes and warriors they named the day,   6825
But Saracen and evil Pagan knaves
Sundered the knot, may Jesus curse their fate!
When all was said as you have heard me say,
See in the hall come messengers in haste
Whom Yon the king, much to be prized and praised,   6830
Has sent from Gascony with tidings grave!
They see the King, first greet him, then proclaim:
"Ah, mighty King, whom all of France obeys,
To your great throne a grievous threat is made!
Fourteen foul kings of evil Pagan race   6835
Have struck in Gascony where they remain!
The city walls of Tarragonne they've razed
And laid to siege Bordeaux on Gironde's wave!
May God, Who judges all of us, gainsay
Your right to rule a fief or realm again,   6840
    If this shame shuns your vengeance!"

189

When all the knights have heard the envoys' speech,
The bravest ones are filled with dread and fear;
Seguin, the count of Bordeaux city, speaks:
"Messenger, brother, is this the truth indeed,   6845
That Saracens have struck inside my fief?"
"Indeed, my lord, the land has been razed clean
And laid to waste and left in direst need;
The first of May is the day they've decreed
To sail their boats across the Gironde's stream,   6850
Whence they shall ride to the town of Orléans,
Then capture Bourges, for they say and they preach
That it was theirs by rights in former years."
"God," says King Charles, "true King of majesty,
Who by the grace of Your goodwill decreed   6855
The crown and rod for me to wear and wield,
Take pity on me now and counsel me
How I may dash the pride of this foul breed
Who have entered my lands most wrongfully;
Advise me now, the wisest of you here,   6860
As you are all my knights and men of liege;

You have been here for a long time at siege
For love of me, I speak this truthfully,
And you have done your service willingly
For the large fiefs I gave you formerly;   6865
Now serve again the King of majesty,
    So you may win His love!"

190

Up on his feet stands swiftly the Archbishop;
He mounts the folding-stool straightway and quickly
And starts to speak in a most noble spirit: 6870
"Barons, my lords, give ear to me and listen:
I stand for God, Who made the world we live in,
And for St. Peter, His regent in Rome city,
To whom He gave the power of forgiveness
To any sinners for any sins committed;   6875
I tell you now that any man who's willing
To go with Charles, keeper of the French kingdom,
Shall be forgiven for a lifetime of sinning,
In Lord God's name, Who made the world we live in."
The French all say: "How high a pardon this is!   6880
How blessèd born all we who shall go with him
    And win so rich a grace!"

191

Up on his feet stands Charlemagne the Emperor;
He calls loudly once more for the attention
Of all his barons and most powerful men there;   6885
He gives them leave and bids them reassemble
Upon the first of May, when summer enters,
Beneath Narbonne in force of arms together,
Whence they shall ride against those faithless felons;
He calls Girart, lord of Vienne, and tells him: 6890
"I go to Spain; you shall remain, protecting
Bavaria and Germany's defenses;
And you, Hernaut of Biaulande, I direct you
To guard Geneva and all its lands appended,
All of Alsace and the town Piacenza,   6895

My fief of Rome, which is called my own center,
And Lombardy, against all misadventure."
"In God's name, sire," the noble Guibourc tells him:
"He trusts you much, who with so much invests you!"
Hernaut replies: "Lady, you speak correctly!"   6900
When this is said, the King mounts up his destrier;
Roland the duke comes into the assembly:
He kisses Aude his lovely bride intended,
And bids her keep his ring in sign and emblem;
And she gives him the beautiful white ensign   6905
Which he used hence so much to show his presence
And rally troops, when in the Spanish empire
He took great towers and made strong towns surrender;
But the foul Moors, God curse them all for ever,
Cleft them apart — that pair were never wedded   6910
And never left an heir for France to treasure;
    Which was a grievous shame.

192

Lords, you have heard of Count Girart the brave
And how his peace was made with Charlemagne;
When all was done as I have sung and named,   6915
King Charles set off into the realm of Spain
And led his host against that evil race
Which had destroyed that part of his domains;
Lords, you have heard the song time and again
How Ganelon betrayed the French that day   6920
When Roland died and all those Peers the same,
And twenty thousand more, God grant them grace,
Whom King Marsile in Roncevaux did slay;
But let us leave those heroes and their fate,
And leave Girart, for I have told his tale,   6925
And Hernaut of Biaulande, the nobly famed;
Of Hernaut's son I'll tell you now, whose name
Was Aymeri, of worth and valor great:
    The liege-lord of Narbonne.

Index of Proper Names

ABILANT: A mountain range in the Anti-Lebanon; identified here with the Sinai Desert, where the Israelites received manna from heaven (Exodus 16:1).

ACHART of Rivier Valley: Father of Garin, Oliver's squire.

ACHATANZ: A Saracen king.

ADAM: The first man (Genesis 2).

AENEAS: Legendary Trojan leader and hero of Virgil's *Aeneid*.

AFLOAIRES: A Saracen king and uncle of Oliver.

AIMART: Nephew of Hernaut of Mongençon and courtier of Charlemagne.

ALBI: Town in the *département* of Tarn in southern France; here the shire of Jocerain, a French knight.

ALEMAN: Inhabitant of Alemannia, a duchy of Charlemagne's extending from Main to Lake Constance and including Alsace.

ALEXANDRIA: Famous city and seaport of Egypt, founded by Alexander the Great in 332 BC. Here, part of the region ruled by Sinagon the Moor.

ALMERIA: Town and region of southeastern Spain; epithet used frequently with "silk" in the *chansons de geste*.

ALSACE: French province, west of the Rhine.

ANJOU: County of medieval France on the Loire river; here, the fief of Geoffrey, Charlemagne's standard-bearer.

APOSTLES (The): The twelve disciples sent forth by Christ to preach the Gospel (Matthew 10:2). The models for Charlemagne's Twelve Peers.

APULIA: Province of southeastern Italy (Puglia). Part of the domain won by Girart's brother Milon.

ARAB: Of Arabia; term used synonymously with Pagan or Saracen in most *chansons de geste*; also a frequent epithet of "steed."

ARAGON: Kingdom of northern Spain; also a frequent epithet of "steed."

AUDE: Daughter of Duke Renier of Geneva, niece of Girart of Vienne and sister of Oliver; becomes the betrothed of Roland.

AUMON: A Saracen prince slain by Roland in the *Chanson d'Aspremont*. First owner of the latter's famous sword Durendal.

AUTEMERE: Unidentified location of the fief of Aymon (q.v.).

AUVERGNE: Ancient county of France whose capital was Clermont-Ferrand.

AYMERI: The son of Hernaut of Biaulande; Girart of Vienne's most fiery-tempered nephew; as Aymeri of Narbonne the hero of his own group of *chansons de geste* and father of William of Orange.

AYMON of Autemere: A French knight.

BALAGUER: A Catalonian stronghold.

BALDWIN (1): An envoy of Charlemagne; companion of Hugh (q.v.); (2): A nephew of Charlemagne.

BAR-SUR-AUBE: Town in the Champagne region of France, where the present work was composed, according to its author Bertrand.

BAVARIA: Ancient duchy annexed to Charlemagne's empire after 800 AD. Legendary fief of Naimes, Charlemagne's beloved counsellor.

BEAUNE: Town in the Côte d'Or region of northeastern France.

BEDOUIN: Nomadic Arab tribes; epithet used synonymously with Pagan or Saracen on occasions.

BERART: The woodsman of Clermont Forest, in the service of Girart.

BERRY: A duchy of medieval France, whose capital was Bourges. Here the fief of Lanbert (q.v.).

BERNART (1): A traitor; (2): A knight in the service of Charlemagne.

BERTHA: The wife of King Pépin and mother of Charlemagne; as "Berthe aux Grand(s) Pied(s)" (Bertha Big-Foot) the heroine of her own *chanson de geste* so titled.

BERTRAND of Bar-sur-Aube: The author of *Girart de Vienne*.

BESANÇON: Town in Franche Comté, eastern France.

BETHLEHEM: Birthplace of Jesus Christ.

BEUVON (1): The (long, white-) bearded duke and ancestor of the Monglane clan; named as Oliver's grandfather in l. 4041 and the ruler of Vienne in his own right in l. 4045 and ll. 5382–86; (2): Son of Girart de Vienne and Guibourc; elder brother of Savariez.

BIAULANDE: The domain of Girart's brother Hernaut; called "Biaulande-on-the-sea" in l. 3712, and identified by G. Paris as the town of Nice.

BORDEAUX: Port on the Gironde; capital of the duchy of Aquitaine.

BOURGES: The capital of Berry (q.v.).

BRIE: Brie-Comte-Robert in the Seine-et-Marne district of northern France.

BRITTANY: Duchy of western France.

BURGUNDY: Ancient kingdom and duchy of France.

CASTILE: Kingdom of northern Spain; epithet used frequently with "steed" in the *chansons de geste*.

CHALON: Town on the Saône river in Burgundy.

CHARLEMAGNE: Charles the Great, King of the Franks (the French), Emperor of France; Uncle of Roland and Baldwin in all *chansons de geste*; here also the godfather of Lanbert of Berry; marries the (unnamed) widow of the duke of Burgundy.

CHÂTILLON: Châtillon-sur-Seine in the Côte-d'Or region of France.

CLERMONT: A forest region near Vienne.

CLOSAMONT: An (imaginary) emperor of Rome, alleged original owner of Oliver's celebrated sword Halteclere.

CLUNY: Abbey town on the Grosne river in Burgundy.

DIDIER of Pavia: King of the Lombards; a knight of Charlemagne, appearing in several *chansons de geste*.

DIJON: Capital of the medieval duchy of Burgundy.

DO of Laon, The bearded: Knight of Charlemagne's court; slain by Aymeri.

DOON of Mayence: Ancestor of the traitor Ganelon; progenitor of Bertrand de Bar's second *geste*, the cycle of the rebel barons.

DROON (1): A knight of Charlemagne; as envoy with Hervi (q.v.) sent to bring Roland and the French army to Charles's aid outside Vienne; (2) DROON of Vincent: An exemplary knight of Charlemagne's court.

DUCHESS (The): The unnamed widow of the duke of Burgundy; promised to Girart, then taken in marriage by Charlemagne, her subsequent humiliation of Girart ignites the smoldering hostility between Duke Girart and his liege.

DURENDAL: The name of Roland's famous sword; first owned by the pagan Prince Aumon (q.v.), whom Roland slays in the epic poem called the *Chanson d'Aspremont*.

EGYPT: Kingdom of northeastern Africa.

ELINANT: Companion of Gautier (3); A knight of Charlemagne (l. 4550) and of Girart (l. 4846)!

ELINÉ: A Greek warrior supposedly slain by Aeneas; first owner of the hauberk given to Oliver by Joachim the Jew.

ELIOT: A knight of Charlemagne's court; slain by Renier.

ENSEIS the Lombard: A knight of Charlemagne; slain by Oliver.

ERMENJART: The wife of Aymeri of Narbonne; the mother of William of Orange.

ESLION: A counsellor of Charlemagne.

EVE: The first woman.

FERRANT: The name of Oliver's horse.

FLANDERS: County of medieval France.

FLEMINGS, FLEMISH: Inhabitants of Flanders; fierce fighters.

FLORI: The name of Ogier the Dane's horse.

FRANCE: Term used to designate either the former Frankish empire of Charlemagne, extending from the Elbe to the Ebro, or the contemporary kingdom as ruled by Louis VII or Philippe-Auguste (and specifically the duchy of France or of Paris).

FRENCH, FRENCHMEN: Inhabitants of France in either designation of the term (q.v.).

FRISIAN: Inhabitants of Frisia, the islands and coast of northeastern Netherlands.

GAIFIER (1): An unidentified king or liege-lord whose name is traditionally linked with great riches or treasures; (2): A duke of Charlemagne; possibly the same as Gaifier (1) (q.v.).

GANELON: A knight of Charlemagne; traditionally a brother-in-law of the Emperor and the step-father of Roland; infamous in the O.F. epics for his betrayal of Roland and the French rear-guard at the Pass of Roncevaux in the Pyrenees; in Bertrand's poem he is said to be a descendant of Doon de Mayence and his *geste* of rebellious barons.

GARIN (1) of Monglane: The father of Hernaut of Biaulande, Milon of Puglia, Renier of Geneva and Girart of Vienne; the grandfather of Aymeri of Narbonne, great-grandfather of William of Orange and progenitor of Bertrand de Bar's third *geste*; (2): The cousin and squire of Oliver.

GASCON: From Gascony (q.v.); frequent epithet of "steed" in the *chansons de geste.*

GASCONY: Old province of southwestern France; named as the location of Monglane.

GAUDIN: the German: A knight of Charlemagne.

GAUDRIS: A knight of Charlemagne.

GAUTIER (1): A deputy provost of Charlemagne's household; (2): The leader of a band of robbers; slain by Aymeri; (3): The companion of

Elinant (q.v.); a knight of Charlemagne.

GAYDON the Old: An exemplary knight of Charlemagne; as Gaydon d'Angers the hero of his own *chanson de geste*.

GENEVA: Situated at the outflow of the Rhône from Lake Geneva in the medieval kingdom of Burgundy; the domain of Girart's brother Renier.

GENÈVRE: A mountain-pass in the Alps between Briançon and Cézane.

GEOFFREY (1) of Anjou: A knight of Charlemagne; (2) of Paris: A knight of Charlemagne.

GERMAN: Of the kingdom of Germany (q.v.).

GERMANY: O. F. *Alemaigne* refered originally to the province of the Alemanni (Alemannia) and later to the entire kingdom of Germany.

GILEBERT: One of a band of robbers slain by Aymeri.

GILEMER: A provost of Charlemagne's household.

GIRART of Vienne: The youngest son of Garin of Monglane; uncle of Oliver, Aude and Aymeri of Narbonne (hence the great-uncle of William of Orange); the husband of Guibourc and father of Beuvon (2) and Savariez; the brother of Hernaut of Biaulande, Milon of Puglia and Renier of Geneva; the hero of the present work.

GIRBERT of Tarragone: A knight of Charlemagne.

GIRONDE: The river in southern France on which Bordeaux is situated.

GUIBOURC: The wife of Girart of Vienne; a sister of King Othon (q.v.).

GUIELIN: Charlemagne's treasurer; slain by Aymeri.

GUIMER: A chaplain of Charlemagne.

GUINEMENT: A knight of Charlemagne; slain by Oliver.

GUION: Girart's gate-keeper in Vienne.

GUIRRÉ: A French archbishop.

HAGUENAN: A knight of Charlemagne; struck down by Milon of Puglia.

HALTECLERE: The name of Oliver's sword, given to him by Joachim the Jew. *See also* CLOSAMONT.

HECTOR: Trojan hero, slain by Achilles.

HELES: The abbot of St. Denis.

HENRY of Orléans: A knight of Charlemagne.

HERMER of Paris: A knight of Charlemagne.

HERNAUT (1) of Biaulande: Eldest son of Garin of Monglane and brother of Girart of Vienne; father of Aymeri of Narbonne (and hence grandfather of William of Orange); (2) HERNAUT of Mongençon: A knight of Charlemagne; (3) HERNAUT the Poitevin: A knight of Charlemagne.

HEROD: The king of Judaea at the time of Christ's birth; responsible for the massacre of the Innocents (Matthew 2:16) (q.v.).

HERVI (1): A citizen of Vienne who lodges the adolescent Girart and Renier; (2): A knight of Charlemagne and companion of Droon (1) (q.v.); struck down by Renier of Geneva.

HUIDELON the Norman: An exemplary knight of Charlemagne.

HUGH: An envoy of Charlemagne; companion of Baldwin (1) (q.v.).

HUNGARY: In all three *chansons de geste* where Girart of Vienne plays a leading role, his wife, although named differently in each poem, is each time said to be closely related to the king of Hungary.

INNOCENTS: The young children of the district of Bethlehem massacred by Herod (q.v.) at the time of Christ's birth (Matthew 2:16).

JERUSALEM: The capital of Judaea. *See also* SALEM.

JESUS: The Christ; the son of God; the second person of the Trinity; His name is often used synonymously with "God" in the *chansons de geste*.

JEWS: The inhabitants of Judaea in the time of Christ; held responsible for His death.

JOACHIM: A Jewish citizen of Vienne.

JOCERAIN of Albi: A knight of Charlemagne; slain by Aymeri of Narbonne.

JONAH: O.T. Prophet who survived three days and nights in the belly of a whale (Matthew 12:40).

JOYEUSE: The name of Charlemagne's sword.

JUDAS: Judas Iscariot; the Apostle who betrayed Christ for thirty pieces of silver (Matthew 26:14).

LANBERT of Berry: A French count captured by Oliver; a godson of Charlemagne and a model of chivalry.

LAON: Ancient city northeast of Soissons; considered (wrongly) in the O.F. epics as a royal city of Charlemagne; the favorite residence of the tenth-century Carolingians.

LENDIT: The location near St. Denis in Paris of a famous fair and holiday celebrating the abbey's relics of the Passion.

LE PERCHE: Ancient county in the province of Maine, northwestern France.

LOMBARDS: Inhabitants of Lombardy (q.v.). Often targets of scorn or humor in the *chansons de geste*.

LOMBARDY: Kingdom of northern Italy conquered by Charlemagne in AD 774.

LONGINUS: The legendary name of the blind centurion who pierced Christ's side on the Cross; according to tradition the blood issuing from the wound restored his sight.

LYON: City on the Rhône in the medieval kingdom of Burgundy.

MÂCON: Cathedral city of medieval Burgundy.

MALQUES of Valsegree: A Pagan who slew the Roman Emperor Closamont (q.v.).

MANESIER: A French count and knight of Charlemagne.

MANIFICANS: An ancient sword-maker, mentioned in more than one *chanson de geste;* said here to have forged Oliver's famous sword Halteclere.

MANS: Town of northern France. In the text a Mans coin is used as a synonym for an item of little value.

MARADANT: A forest location where the French knight Roboant is said here to have slain Aeneas and gained his wondrous suit of armor, worn subsequently by Oliver.

MARNE: River of Champagne region, northern France.

MARSILE: The infamous Saracen king of Saragossa, slain by Roland in the *Chanson de Roland.*

MARSONE: Unidentified location (from the context probably in southern France) of the fief of the father-in-law of Hernaut of Biaulande.

(MARY) MAGDALEN: Identified in the tradition of the Church with the Mary, sister of Martha and Lazarus of Bethany (John 11:2), "who was a sinner." Luke records that she washed Christ's feet with her tears.

MILAN: Major city of Lombardy, northern Italy.

MILES (MILON) of Puglia: Elder brother of Girart of Vienne.

MONGLANE: Unidentified location of the domain of Lord Garin, the father of Girart; said by the poet to be both in Gascony and on the banks of the Rhône!

MONTPELLIER: Chief city of the Hérault district of southern France; frequently cited in the *chansons de geste* as an epithet of "gold" or "shoes," and as an indicator of great distance in the expression "from here to Montpellier."

MORANT (1): The abbot of Cluny monastery; (2): A bishop of Vienne.

MOREHEIER: A knight of Girart.

MOSES: The O.T. prophet.

MOUNTJOY: The war-cry of the French.

NAIMES: A duke of Bavaria; Charlemagne's closest friend and wisest counsellor.

NARBONNE: Capital of Carolingian *Septimania*, now the chief town of the Aude *département*, southern France; famous seat of Aymeri, Girart's nephew and father of William of Orange.

NERO'S FIELD(S): The medieval *pratum/prata Neronis*; site of the *circus Neronis* in Rome, the traditional place of St. Peter's martyrdom and the present-day site of the Vatican.

NEUVILLE: Fortified location in the *département* of Rhône, between Vienne and Lyons.

NEVELON: A nephew of Girart.

NORMAN: Inhabitant of Normandy.

NORMANDY: Medieval duchy of northern France.

NORSE: Of ancient Scandinavia, especially Norway.

NORWEGIAN: Of Norway; used somewhat originally in this poem, together with Norse, as an epithet of "steed."

OGIER: A Danish duke and, after Roland, Charlemagne's bravest knight; the hero of his own group of *chansons de geste*.

OLIVER: Son of Renier of Geneva, brother of Aude and nephew of Girart de Vienne; Roland's beloved companion in the *Chanson de Roland* and other O.F. epics; the finest flower of French knighthood, a paragon of courtesy and bravery.

ORLÉANS: Ancient capital of the duchy of Orléans on the Loire; considered a royal city.

OTHON: A king and brother of Girart's wife Guibourc.

OTON: A knight of Charlemagne, slain by Hernaut of Biaulande.

OTTO: A Bavarian duke and knight of Charlemagne.

PALATRE's ford: An unidentified location near Beaune (q.v.).

PALERMO: Sea-port of northern Sicily; part of the domain won by Girart's brother Miles of Puglia.

PARADISE: Heaven of the Christian Church.

PARIS (1): Capital of the kingdom of France; principal seat of Charlemagne in the present poem; (2): In Greek mythology the son of Priam, king of Troy, and Hecuba.

PAVIA: Capital of the kingdom of Lombardy; frequent epithet of "helm" in the *chansons de geste*.

PENTECOST: Festival of the Christian Church held on the seventh Sunday after Easter (Whit Sunday), commemorating the descent of the Holy Spirit upon Christ's disciples on the day of the Jewish Pentecost.

PÉPIN: Pépin the short, the father of Charlemagne.

PIACENZA: Town in northern Italy.

PILATE: Pontius Pilate of the Gospels; considered as a Saracen god in the *chansons de geste*; one medieval legend describes the imprisonment of Pilate in Vienne itself.

POINÇONET: A young knight of Girart; slain by Roland.

POITIERS: Capital of the medieval county of Poitou.

PONTHIEU: Town in the Somme region of northern France.

POPE (The): Patriarch of Western Christendom.

PRIAM: In Greek legend the king of Troy.

PUGLIA: Province of southeastern Italy; part of the domain won by Girart's brother Miles (of Puglia). *See also* APULIA.

RENART of Pevier: A knight of Charlemagne hostile at court to Girart and Renier.

RENIER (1): The archbishop of Besançon; RENIER (2) of Geneva: Third son of Garin of Monglane; brother of Girart of Vienne; father of Oliver and Aude.

RHEIMS: Cathedral city in Champagne.

RHÔNE (The): River of southeastern France on which Vienne is situated.

RICHARD of Normandy: A duke of Charlemagne's court.

ROBOANT: French knight alleged to have slain Aeneas (q.v.).

ROLAND: The beloved nephew of Charlemagne and his bravest, proudest knight; step-son of Ganelon; becomes in this poem the companion of Oliver and the betrothed of Aude.

ROME: See of the Pope.

ROMAGNA: Ancient province of northern Italy.

RONCEVAUX: The junction of two roads in the Pyrenees on the route between St. Jean-Pied-de-Port and Pampeluna. The scene of the ambush of Charlemagne's rear-guard in 778, and the location of the pitched battle in the *Chanson de Roland* where Roland, Oliver, the Twelve Peers and all Charlemagne's rear-guard are slain through the treachery of Ganelon.

ST. DENIS (1): The martyr Dionysius, first bishop of Paris (third century); as St. Denis, the patron of France and of the royal abbey near

Paris; (2): The town and more specifically the abbey north of Paris which was the sacred resting-place of French kings and the depository of the Oriflamme, their battle-standard.

ST. ELIJAH: The O.T. prophet venerated on July 20.

ST. JAMES: The apostle whose shrine was at Santiago de Compostela in Galicia (Spain).

ST. JOHN's Feast: The feast of the nativity of St. John the Baptist on June 24.

ST. LAZARUS: The brother of Martha and Mary who was raised from the dead by Jesus (John 11).

ST. LEONARD: St. Leonard of Noblac.

ST. MARY: The blessèd Virgin; the mother of Jesus Christ; the intercessor for sinners with Him.

ST. MAUR-DES-FOSSÉES: Town to the east of Paris in the Seine *département*

ST. MAURICE (1): The commander of the Theban Legion martyred under Diocletian in the canton Valais; (2): The cathedral of St. Maurice at Vienne; (3): The name of Girart de Vienne's battle-standard and hence the war-cry of his troops.

ST. MÉDARD: Bishop of Noyon (died c. 557).

ST. PETER: The leader of Christ's Twelve Apostles, martyred in Rome under Nero.

ST. PETER's: The name of the basilica in Rome.

ST. RÉMY: Remigius, the archbishop of Rheims who converted King Clovis.

ST. RIQUIER: The seventh-century hermit of Centule in Picardy.

ST. SIMEON: The Simeon of the Gospels, who held Jesus in his arms in the temple (Luke 2:25).

ST. SIMON: The apostle Simon.

ST. STEPHEN (the shrine of): The cathedral of St. Stephen at Sens.

SALEM: Jerusalem (q.v.).

SAMSON: The biblical Israelite hero of mighty strength (Judges 13–15); the tradition of Samson's wealth appears in more than one *chanson de geste*.

SAVARIEZ: The younger son of Girart de Vienne and Guibourc; the brother of Beuvon.

SEA of Ice: Mythical frozen sea near Iceland.

SEGUIN of Bordeaux: A count of Charlemagne.

SENLIS: Town north of Paris in the Oise *département*.

SENS: Cathedral city southeast of Paris.

SERVAL: An unidentified location between St. Denis and Senlis.

SICILY: Here a duchy of Miles of Puglia.

SIMON: Simon the Pharisee (Luke 7:36–50).

SINAGON: A Saracen king of Alexandria who invades Garin of Monglane.

SOLOMON: The O.T. king of Israel; built the temple at Jerusalem.

SYRIA: Ancient country at the east end of the Mediterranean; epithet used frequently with "mule" and "destrier" in the *chansons de geste*.

TARENTAISE: A district in the Savoie region of eastern France.

TARRAGONE: The town and region of Tarragona, northeastern Spain.

TOULOUSE: Chief town of Haute Garonne, southern France.

TROY: Ancient city on the Scamander river in northwest Asia Minor; besieged by the Greeks in the Trojan war.

VALSORE: An unidentified Saracen town.

VAUDON: An unidentified river between Chalon-sur-Sâone and Vienne.

VERMANDOIS: County of medieval France whose capital was Saint-Quentin; today a region extending through the *départements* of Aisne and Somme.

VESPASIAN: Emperor of Rome 69–79 AD.

VIANA: Town of northwestern Spain.

VIENNE: Town of Isère in the Dauphiné, southwestern France; domain of Girart.

VIRGIN (The Blessèd): St. Mary (q.v.), the Mother of Christ.

YON: The king of Gascony.